A Reference Guide to

Texas Law and Legal History

Sources and Documentation

A Reference Guide to Texas Law and Legal History

Sources and Documentation

by Marian Boner

University of Texas Press, Austin & London

Publication of this book was assisted by the
University of Texas Law School Foundation

Library of Congress Cataloging in Publication Data

Boner, Marian, 1909–
A reference guide to Texas law and legal history.
Includes index.
1. Legal research—Texas. 2. Law—Texas—History and criticism. I. Title.
KFT1275.B65 340'.09764 75-19408
ISBN 0-292-77007-3

Printed in the United States of America

To Helen Hargrave

whose career as teacher, librarian, and scholar
has influenced the legal research of generations
of Texas lawyers

Contents

Preface

During the years spent in law school most students necessarily learn to deal with the basic sources of law. Whether or not the school offers formal instruction in legal research, some knowledge of statutes and reports, encyclopedias and digests is acquired. It is rare, however, that anything beyond a general survey is attempted in the legal education process. The idiosyncracies of different jurisdictions remain obscure to the student, and the attorney who needs occasional information on out-of-state sources quite often has none available.

This book will attempt to supply some of the lacking information for research in Texas law, in both the current and the historical aspects. It is taken for granted that readers will have a fundamental grasp of the ordinary legal sources and how to use them; this is in no sense a textbook for legal bibliography. Discussion will be limited to the points peculiar to this state. Bibliographies are offered for those interested in further research, but they do not purport to be exhaustive.

My research for the book began while I was a member of the faculty and the library staff at the University of Texas School of Law. Much of it could not have been written without the help and encouragement of my colleagues. The first chapter was developed from historical materials compiled by Professor Helen Hargrave for the course in legal bibliography; the chapter on legislative history derives from Professor Millard Ruud's memorandum, "Extrinsic Aids to Interpretation of Texas Statutes," prepared for his classes in legislation. Mr. James Sanders and his staff at the Legislative Reference Library contributed information to bring this article up to date. Associate Justice Jack Pope of the Texas Supreme Court contributed personal advice to supplement the contents of his scholarly opinions. To all those who shared their expertise so generously, I offer grateful acknowledgement, assuming responsibility for any errors in transferring their information to the pages of the book.

Thanks are due also to the State Bar of Texas for permission to reproduce the Writ of Error Table which appears in Chapter 7 (from the article by Simpson, *Notations on Applications for Writs of Error, Texas Bar Journal*, vol. 12, no. 11 [December 1949]), and to Texas Law Review Publications, Inc., for permission to use the material in the citation guide, *Texas Rules of Form* (Appendix D).

1. Historical Background

We are frequently reminded, by the state itself and by commercial enterprises, that at different times in its history Texas has been governed "under six flags"—those of France, Spain, Mexico, the Republic of Texas, the Confederate States, and the United States. The legal history of the state carries many reminders of the same fact. Although French law left few permanent traces, the Spanish civil law and its Mexican derivative are woven into the fabric of the Texas legal system, forming a true seamless web with the common law of the Anglo-Americans who later colonized the territory.

The first true Spanish code, Las Siete Partidas, was compiled late in the thirteenth century but was not promulgated until 1348. Nearly two hundred years later, in 1530, its authority was extended to the New World by its incorporation into the Recopilación de las Leyes de Indias.[1] Later compilations superseded but did not repeal the Partidas, and its provisions were considered to be still in force in Texas until the reception of the common law by the Act of 1840. It was cited frequently in early Texas cases, and its influence is still seen in this state and in others with Spanish backgrounds.[2]

To a great extent the provisions of the Partidas were derived from Roman law and marked its first reception in Spain. Concepts of the canon law, the maritime law of the period, and the native customs and laws of the Spanish provinces were incorporated in it. It included also some elements of the Visigothic Code of A.D. 480, the source of our community property system.

Later compilations of laws were never extended to the colonies as a whole, although parts of them were designated as particularly for the overseas possessions. Even the Novísima Recopilación was never in force as an entity; the Mexican Supreme Court has restricted its scope to those provisions intended for promulgation in the Indies.[3] The Cedulario Indiano of 1596, however, and the Recopilación de Leyes de los Reynos de las Indias in 1681 were strictly colonial legislation, as were the Ordenanzas de Minería de Nueva España in 1779. Legislation for the Indies originated in many diverse agencies and, in general, was restricted to public law. Questions of private law were settled by reference to the laws of Spain.

By the nineteenth century, Texas was still little more than a vague territory lying between New Spain and New France. Spanish efforts at colonization had not been successful, and the government was pleased to grant to Moses Austin—and later to his son Stephen—the right to bring in Anglo-American settlers. Texas legal history proper begins with Stephen F. Austin's colonization laws of 1822.

Austin at first governed his colony in person, with a provisional justice of the peace to serve in his absence. In 1824 he issued a set of "Instructions and Regulations" which provided a kind of civil and criminal code for the colony. (See David B. Gracy, *Establishing Austin's Colony,* p. 75.) They were a curious blend of common law and civil law, in which *alcaldes* and *alguaciles* shared jurisdiction with constables and justices of the peace. This unorthodox legal system was well adapted to the frontier society for which it was designed, and it contained many features that were kept in later codes.

At various times while under Mexican rule, Texas was combined with other areas for purposes of local government. Only one such government is relevant for most research: the state of Coahuila and Texas, formed in the first year of Mexico's independence from Spain. This unit was governed, like any other part of Mexico, under its own constitution and that of the federal government. The Ordinances and Decrees of Coahuila and Texas are a standard source and may be found in many libraries. They are reproduced in the first volume of *Gammel's Laws* (H. P. N. Gammel, *Laws of Texas 1822-1897*), along with many others of the colonial period.

Since Coahuilans outnumbered Texans by at least three to one, it was natural that the constitution and laws should follow Spanish precedents. The federal Constitution of 1824 lacked the provisions for trial by jury, freedom of religion, and other rights that were familiar and important to the settlers. After Santa Anna overthrew the 1824 constitution, the Texans made a halfhearted attempt to restore it, which was soon abandoned. In 1835 a provisional government was set up under the Ordinances and Decrees of the Consultation at San Felipe,[4] which may be called the first truly Texan—or Texian[5]—legal document.

Even today it is frequently necessary to refer to the early Spanish and Mexican sources in cases concerning land grants, water rights, and minerals. Texas land grants derive from four different sovereigns: Spain, up to 1821; Mexico, from 1821 through 1835; the Republic of Texas, from 1836 to 1845; and the state, from that time on. But note that the land south of the Nueces River was part of the state of Tamaulipas, not of Coahuila and Texas. It was not until December 19, 1836, that the Congress extended the Texas claims to the Rio Grande, and Mexico did not acknowledge the claims until the Treaty of Guadalupe Hidalgo in 1848. These facts add further complications to the study of Texas land titles.

Contrary to its position in other states, the United States has never held title to any public lands in Texas. The documents effecting the annexation of Texas reserved all public lands to the state.[6] Each grant must be examined in the light of the appropriate laws as of the time it was made, and the constitutions and treaties of succeeding sovereigns must be checked to determine the exact provisions honoring grants from previous governments.

Most of the essential sources are available in English translation, as listed in the bibliography for this chapter. Occasionally it is necessary to delve into archival sources, which becomes more difficult. Collections at the State Library, at the University of Texas, and in Bexar County have been organized to minimize this difficulty, and guides have been published to assist in their use (see the works by Castaneda, Kielman, and Taylor in the bibliography for this chapter).

It should be noted that different editions of the same work may offer varying interpretations of the law. Escriche, for example, whose *Diccionario razonado* is an excellent source, published a revised edition while he was living in France. This edition was strongly influenced by the Napoleonic Code, some concepts of which are not in accord with Spanish law. For this reason the editions published in Madrid are to be preferred.

Notes

1. Oddly enough, this span of years corresponds almost exactly to the period covered by the Year Books which laid the foundations of the English common law:1289–1535.

2. See, for example, the opinions of Garwood, J., in Luttes v. State, 159 Tex. 500, 324 S.W.2d 167 (1958), and Pope, J., in State of Texas v. Valmont Plantations, 346 S.W.2d 853 (Tex. Civ. App.—San Antonio 1961), aff'd and opinion adopted, 163 Tex. 381, 355 S.W.2d 502 (1962).

3. Manuel Z. de la Garza, 5 Semanario (2a época) 1, July 1, 1882. Some confusion seems to exist about the name of the

case; logically it would seem to be Patricio Milmo, and it is sometimes cited as Garza v. Milmo.

4. One of the documents reprinted in vol. 1 of *Gammel's Laws.*

5. A word popularized by the late J. Frank Dobie to characterize the hardy pioneer era of Texas history. It was in common use at the time of the republic.

6. Joint Res. March 1, 1845 (5 Stat. 797); Joint Res. for Annexing Texas to the United States (Convention) July 4, 1845, in 2 H. GAMMEL, LAWS OF TEXAS 1226 (1898).

Bibliography

Blackmar, Frank W. *Spanish Institutions of the Southwest.* Studies in Historical and Political Science, extra vol. 10. Baltimore: Johns Hopkins University Press, 1891.

Castaneda, Carlos. Spanish Archives in San Antonio, Texas. M.A. thesis, University of Texas, 1923.

Cedulario Indiano: Reproducción facsimil de la ed. única de 1596. 4 vols. Madrid: Ediciones Cultura Hispánica, 1945–1946.

códigos españoles, Los. 12 vols. Madrid: Impr. de la Publicidad, 1847–1851. Contains the early quasi-codes, such as the Fuero Juzgo and Fuero Real, as well as the Siete Partidas and its successors.

Colección de los decretos y órdenes de las cortes de España que se reputan vigentes en la República de los Estados Unidos Mexicanos. Mexico City: Impr. de Galván, 1829.

Colón de Larriátegui, Felix. *Juzgados militares de España y sus Indias.* 3d ed. 4 vols. Madrid: Impr. de Repullés, 1817.

Dobkins, Betty Eakle. *The Spanish Element in Texas Water Law.* Austin: University of Texas Press, 1959.

Elizondo, Francisco de Antonio de. *Práctica universal forense de los tribunales de España y de las Indias.* 8 vols. Madrid: Ibarra, 1783-1791.

Escriche y Martín, Joaquín. *Diccionario razonado de legislación civil, penal, comercial y forense.* 4 vols. Madrid: Impr. de E. Cuesta, 1874-1876.

Franquet y Bertran, Cirilo. *Ensayo sobre el origen, espíritu y progresos de la legislación de las aguas.* 2 vols. Madrid: Ducazcal, 1864.

Galván Rivera, Mariano. *Ordenanzas de tierras y aguas.* 5th ed. Paris: Rosa y Bouret, 1856.

Gamboa, Francisco Xavier de. *Commentaries on the Mining Ordinances of Spain.* Translated by Richard Heathfield. 2 vols. London: Longman, Rees, Orme, Brown and Green, 1830.

Gammel, H. P. N. *Laws of Texas 1822-1897.* 10 vols. Austin, 1898. Volume 1 includes:

Austin's Colonization Laws, 1822
Constitution of 1824
Federal Colonization Law, 1824
Colonization Law, Coahuila and Texas, 1825
Fredonian Declaration of Independence, 1826
Laws and Decrees, State of Coahuila and Texas, 1824
Constitution, State of Coahuila and Texas, 1827
Colonization Law, State of Tamaulipas, 1826
Naturalization Law of the General Congress, 1828
San Felipe Convention, 1832
Journals of the Consultation [at San Felipe], 1835
Proceedings of the General Council, 1835-1836
Goliad Declaration of Independence, 1835
Journals of the Convention at Washington, 1836
Ordinances and Decrees of the Consultation [at San Felipe], 1836 [includes the Plan and Powers of the Provisional Government of Texas]

Declaration of Independence, 1836
Constitution of the Republic, 1836

Gracy, David B. *Establishing Austin's Colony.* Austin: Pemberton Press, 1970.

Hall, Frederic. *The Laws of Mexico.* San Francisco: Bancroft, 1885.

Hamilton, Leonidas. *Mexican Law.* San Francisco, 1882.

Hawkins, Walace. *El sal del rey* [in English]. Austin: State Historical Association, 1947.

Kielman, Chester V., comp. *The University of Texas Archives: A Guide to the Historical Manuscripts Collection in The University of Texas Library.* Austin: University of Texas Press, 1968.

Moreau Lislet, L., and Henry Carleton. *The Laws of Las Siete Partidas.* 2 vols. New Orleans, 1820.

New Laws of the Indies . . . facsimile reprint of original with translation in the English language. London: Chiswick Press, 1893.

Novísima Recopilación de las Leyes de España. 6 vols. Madrid: J. Viana Razola, 1829.

Ordenanzas de Minería de Nueva España. Paris: C. Bouret, 1881.

Pandectas Hispano-Megicanas. 3 vols. Mexico City: Impr. Galván Rivera, 1839-1840.

Recopilación de Leyes de los Reynos de las Indias. 4 vols. 2d ed. Madrid: A. Balbas, 1756.

Reynolds, Matthew G. *Spanish and Mexican Land Laws.* Saint Louis: Buston and Louis, 1895.

Rockwell, John A. *Compilation of Spanish and Mexican Law Relating to Mines and Titles to Real Estate.* New York: Voorhis, 1851.

Schmidt, Gustavus. *The Civil Law of Spain and Mexico.* New Orleans: Rea, 1851.

Scott, Samuel Parsons, ed. and trans. *Las Siete Partidas.* Chicago: Commerce Clearing House, 1931.

——. *The Visigothic Code.* Boston: Boston Book Co., 1910.

Smith, Bennett. *Marriage by Bond in Colonial Texas.* Fort Worth: Branch-Smith, 1972.

Taylor, Virginia H. *The Spanish Archives of the General Land Office of Texas.* Austin: Lone Star Press, 1955.

Vance, John T. *The Background of Hispano-American Law.* New York: Central, 1942.

Ware, Eugene. *Roman Water Law.* Saint Paul: West, 1905.

White, Joseph M. *A New Collection of Laws . . . of Great Britain, France and Spain relating to the concession of lands, with the laws of Mexico and Texas on the same subject.* 2 vols. Philadelphia: T. and J. W. Johnson, 1839. Frequently bound with the spine title *Land Laws of California, Oregon and Texas* and generally called by land lawyers *White's New Recopilación.*

Wooten, Dudley G. *A Comprehensive History of Texas.* 2 vols. Dallas: Scarff, 1898. Volume 1 is a reprint of Yoakum's history; see below.

Wortham, Louis J. *History of Texas.* 5 vols. Fort Worth: Wortham and Molyneux, 1924.

Yoakum, Henderson K. *History of Texas from Its First Settlement to . . . 1846.* Facsimile reprint. Austin: Steck, 1935. Also reprinted as the first volume of Wooten's history; see above.

2. Constitutions

In 1836 the new republic adopted a constitution to succeed the provisional document drafted by the Consultation at San Felipe. As was to be expected, it bore a strong resemblance to that of the United States, based on a separation of powers and a bill of rights. Many of its clauses reflect the two concepts that permeate the body of Texas law—dependence on the common law, plus a recognition that in some respects the Spanish system is to be preferred. A good example is the clause instructing the Congress to introduce the common law of England, with such modifications as might be thought desirable. Accordingly, in 1840 an act was passed marking the reception of the common law,[1] but excepting from its coverage all land grants, mineral rights, and marital-property concepts. In these areas and in the system of courts and pleadings, the civil law prevailed.

The Constitution of 1845 differed only slightly from that of 1836, merely introducing the adjustments necessary in changing from the status of a republic to that of a state. An ordinance limiting and regulating colonization was enacted on the same day that saw the adoption of the constitution; this document has been held to be of equal force with the constitution itself.[2]

In 1861 a similar constitution effected the withdrawal from the Union and the change to the Confederacy, and in 1866 another signaled the supposed restoration of federal status. This latter document did not meet with approval by the United States Congress and had little effect. The officers acting under it were removed by the military government, and new ones were appointed. Texas was readmitted to the Union under the Constitution of 1869, which was superseded in 1876 by the present one.

The texts of all these documents are easily found. They are reproduced in the volumes of *Gammel's Laws* covering the appropriate years; they were collected and annotated by several authors; and they are all reproduced in the third volume of Vernon's *Constitution of the State of Texas Annotated*, a part of the "Black Statutes." The same volume contains an excellent history of the various constitutions, reprinted from Sayles's *Constitutions of the State of Texas*. The annotations in this volume provide a very good legislative history of the provisions, plus an interpretive commentary following each section. These commentaries sometimes amount to substantial articles.[3]

The present constitution, drafted in 1875 and adopted the following year, is a long and verbose document, dealing at length with matters ordinarily left to legislation. As a consequence, amendments have been frequent and lavish. Its minute detailing is usually explained as a reaction against the arbitrary actions of the Reconstruction government and a resulting determination that nothing should be left to the discretion of future officials. All amendments, whether adopted or merely proposed by the legislature, are listed in a cumulative table which appears in each volume of the session laws, with references to the volume where the language of the amendment appears.

There have been increasingly frequent plans for constitutional revision in the past two decades, but so far all have proven fruitless. A constitutional convention met in 1974, with the Sixty-third Legislature acting as convention delegates, but failed to adopt a draft to submit to the voters of the state. There are several different plans for continuing its work in the Sixty-fourth Legislature, some of which may bear fruit.

Notes

1. An act to adopt the common law of England . . . January 20, 1840. Laws of the Republic of Texas 1 (Fourth Congress), 2 H. GAMMEL, LAWS OF TEXAS 177 (1898).

2. Stewart v. Crosby, 15 Tex. 545 (1856).

3. See, for example, that on homestead law, a Texas innovation, in vol. 3 at p. 320.

Bibliography

Bell, Hollond E. The Texas Convention of 1832. M.A. thesis, University of Texas, 1907.

Braden, George D. *Citizens' Guide to the Texas Constitution.* Austin, 1972. Prepared for the Texas Advisory Commission on Intergovernmental Relations, by the Institute for Urban Studies, University of Houston.

Constitutions of the State of Texas Annotated. 3 vols. Kansas City: Vernon, 1955.

Gammel, H. P. N. *Laws of Texas 1822–1897.* 10 vols. Austin, 1898.

Huey, Mary E. *Texas Constitutional Revision.* Dallas: Arnold Foundation, 1962.

Journal of the Consultation Held at San Felipe de Austin. Houston: Telegraph Press, 1838. Reprinted in 1 *Gammel's Laws of Texas.*

Journals of the Convention Assembled . . . on the Fourth of July 1845. Austin: Miner and Cruger, 1845. Reprint, Austin: Shoal Creek Publishers, 1974.

Journals of the Proceedings of the General Council of the Republic of Texas Held at San Felipe de Austin. Houston:

National Intelligencer Office, 1839. Reprinted in 1 *Gammel's Laws of Texas.*

Journals of the Secession Convention of Texas, 1861. Austin: Austin Printing Company, 1912. Facsimile.

McKay, Seth Shepard. *Making the Texas Constitution of 1876.* Ph.D. thesis, University of Pennsylvania, 1924.

——. *Seven Decades of the Texas Constitution of 1876.* Lubbock, 1942.

——, ed. *Debates in the Texas Constitutional Convention of 1875.* Austin: University of Texas, 1930.

Rowland, Walton C. Amendments to the Texas Constitution, 1876–1948. M.A. thesis, University of Texas, 1948.

Sayles, John. *Constitutions of the State of Texas . . . Annotated.* 4th ed. Saint Louis: Gilbert, 1893.

Texas, Citizens Advisory Committee on Revision of the Constitution of Texas. *Report.* Austin, 1959.

Texas, Constitutional Revision Commission. *Reports and Recommendations to the . . . 61st Legislature.* Austin, 1968.

Texas State Library, Legislative Reference Division. *Amendments to the Constitution of 1876.* Austin, 1956.

Weeks, William F., Reporter. *Debates of the Texas Convention.* Houston: Cruger, 1846.

3. Legislation

Texas session laws have been published regularly under both the republic and the state. Original copies are quite rare for the early years, and the standard source is a reprint, Gammel's *Laws of Texas 1822–1897.* The first volume contains all of the pre-republic documents, including many of purely historical interest as well as the laws, constitutions, treaties, and others of legal nature.[1] Later volumes of the set contain all of the laws and constitutions for the years covered and are identical with the originals, including pagination.

Gammel continued to publish unofficial editions of Texas laws for several years after the turn of the century, simply adding to the official edition a title page bearing his imprint. (He was also the printer for the official version.) For these years, therefore, some copies may be bound as *Gammel's Laws* while others lack this designation; the contents do not differ. However, the set called *Gammel's Laws* consists of only the first ten volumes, or perhaps the first twelve. The inclusion of the two extra volumes is due to the publication in 1906 of two very good indexes covering all twelve.[2] After this date there is no cumulative index to the Texas session laws.

The legislature meets regularly in the odd-numbered years and frequently is called into extra sessions. The general and special laws of all sessions have been published, in various combinations or separately, according to the preference of the current secretary of state. Since about 1941 there has been no attempt to classify the laws as general or special, and they are published in a standard format, usually with the sessions of one legislature composing a single volume. The West Publishing Company has undertaken the publication.

There is no official publication of slip laws, but current legislation is available from several sources. *Vernon's Texas Session Law Service* (now published by West) provides a standard form of the laws, in advance sheet form, paged as they will appear in the bound volume.[3] References are furnished for the prospective citation in *Vernon's Texas Revised Statutes Annotated* (also called *Vernon's Annotated Civil and Criminal Statutes of the State of Texas*). A period of about six weeks elapses between passage of a law and its publication.

The Commerce Clearing House *Texas Advance Session Law Reports* makes copies of the acts available immediately after enactment but lacks the organizational features of the Vernon service. Various Austin firms offer current services on different phases of legislative and governmental activities, and copies of laws may be obtained from them. They are discussed more fully in the next chapter.

The Constitutions of 1836 and 1845 provided that as soon as possible the laws should be collected and codified, but there was considerable delay in starting the project. In the meantime, several unofficial compilations appeared. The first was Dallam's *Digest of the Laws of Texas.* Published in 1845, it contained a digest of the laws plus decisions of the Supreme Court of the Republic. This *Digest* was both incomplete and confusing. It paraphrased the more important laws passed by the Congress but had no verbatim language; moreover, some laws were cited without even being summarized. And, since Dallam seems to have considered Blackstone's *Commentaries* to be of at least equal authority with the Texas laws, an unwary user may confuse one with the other. Dallam's work has little interest except for historians.

Hartley tried in 1850 to produce a more usable digest but succeeded only in providing a more voluminous one. Nine years later the legislature commissioned Oldham and White to compile an official edition, but it was no more satisfactory than its predecessors. The first really successful one was compiled by George Paschal and was first published in 1866.

Paschal was one of the more colorful figures of the Texian era. He disagreed wholeheartedly with his state's actions on secession and war, and he spent the Civil War years working on his digests of statutes and decisions. His plan, stated in the preface, provided for giving the "old law, the mischief and the remedy, in the same view." That is, he printed the law in force, the repealed law or a note of the change, and the judicial construction of both, in close connection. The use of different type faces for these three features gave a clear view of the development of the law and contributed to making Paschal's *Digest* the authoritative, if not quite the official, book for Texas lawyers. The third edition appeared in two volumes, the second being supplemental to a reprint of the volume published as the second edition. The fourth and fifth editions inserted supplementary pages into the second volume instead of revising it.

The author, never one to underestimate his own achievements, said that his work would "be a necessity as long as Texas jurisprudence shall endure." He may have been right; the state's current statutes trace their history to the sections in his *Digest*, and for some research the later editions are still useful. For example, his impassioned account of the Semicolon Case and its accompanying events (discussed in Chapter 5 below) is one of the best sources for this historical oddity. It is found at pages 1393e *et seq.* of the fourth edition.

The last important unofficial compilation was the Sayles' *Early Laws of Texas*. It included most of the early laws covered by Gammel's edition, and added the land and colonization laws of Spain and Mexico, as well as a summary of Spanish civil law. The omission of many laws limits its usefulness, and the lack of the original paging detracts also from its value. Nevertheless, it is an important source for land title research. It provides a history of the municipal divisions of the state, with boundaries of all the colonies and of the early counties. Also included are a glossary of terms used in the old surveys and land grants, and a table of land measures. This last is of great use to out-of-state lawyers lacking familiarity with the vara, the hacienda, and the league-and-labor.[4]

Meanwhile, realizing that the laws had become unusable, the legislature in 1854 authorized a revision and appointed a commission to do the codification. The commissioners did in fact draft four codes: procedural and substantive, for both civil and criminal law. Only two of these, the Penal Code and the Code of Criminal Procedure, were adopted. They are known as the Codes of 1856, or sometimes simply the Old Code, and for many years were the only official compiled laws of the state.

The legislation of this period, in Texas perhaps more than in any other jurisdiction, was much influenced by Edward Livingston's work in Louisiana. His procedural code, designed to replace the tangle of French and Spanish law then prevailing, was so impressive in its simplicity that the Texas Commission of 1854 followed his example, rejecting both the complicated common-law forms of action and the pure Spanish system. The Livingston codes were never adopted in Louisiana, but his introduction and explanation became classics in their field, and no research in this period can ignore them. The commission's report has been of value also, particularly for the recent work on revision of the Texas Penal Code, finally adopted by the Sixty-third Legislature.

Texas constitutions continued their mandate for codification, and in 1879 the legislature adopted the first complete official revision. It was based principally on the fifth edition of Paschal's *Digest* and indicated by marginal notes the *Digest* section (P.D._) furnishing the source for each article so derived. The report of the commissioners who revised the laws gives a detailed history of many provisions, with reasons for the changes made. This report was published officially and nearly fifty years later was reprinted in the *Texas Law Review*.[5]

Subsequent revisions took place in 1895, 1911, and 1925. The last of these is to a large extent still in force, although many sections have been recompiled and revised to provide separate codes on various fields of law. An ongoing program of revision, supervised by the Legislative Council, has produced several codes of this type, and the work is expected to continue until the 1925 revision is completely replaced. After a code is completed, considerable time may elapse before it is made into bound volumes as part of the set.

The first set of annotated statutes was published by the Sayles in 1888. It was kept up to date by supplementary volumes well into the present century; but before the 1911 revision the copyright was bought by a publisher, and in 1914 an edition called *Vernon's Sayles* appeared. With the 1925 revision the Sayles' name was dropped, and *Vernon's Texas Revised Statutes Annotated* was published—the familiar "Black Statutes," so called because of the black binding. For over forty years Vernon served as a quasi-official publisher of Texas laws, before being absorbed by West Publishing Company in 1969.

The original twenty-six volumes of annotated statutes have grown into a set of about ninety, including those that contain the Constitution, Penal Code, Code of Criminal Procedure, Rules of Civil Procedure, and an index covering all of them. They are kept up to date with annual pocket parts and quarterly supplements, and a session law service is published while the legislature is in session. The annotations, like those of other

West publications, provide references to law reviews and to *Corpus Juris Secundum* sections in addition to cases and attorney-general opinions. Historical notes furnish information on changes in content and phraseology over the years.

There has been no official edition of the statutes since that of 1925, the Vernon set being for all practical purposes the only one available. Vernon also published an unannotated Centennial Edition in 1936 (the anniversary of Texas independence) and another unannotated compilation in 1948. These were not new revisions, but merely recompilations of all articles still in force from the 1925 version. Biennial supplements for the 1948 edition were published through 1974, with each supplement representing the work of one legislature. These "Red Statutes"—again, from the color of the binding—were bulky and inconvenient, lacking any cumulative index, and were seldom used except to locate repealed statutes not in the current annotated volumes. In 1974 a new compilation similar to the 1948 version appeared (*West's Texas Statutes and Codes*); in all probability it will suffer from the same defects as its predecessor, since the publisher has announced that it will be supplemented in similar fashion. However, it will offer the advantage of supplying in organized form the new codes and their auxiliary but uncodified laws. The set is bound in green but is too new to have acquired a nickname.

Tracing the origin of a section of the statutes is usually quite simple. Each article of every revision carries, in addition to its own number, the numbers of the equivalent article in each preceding revision, with the earliest one last. A complete record of the session law origin and any later amendments appears at the end of the article. The 1879 revision, as stated above, refers for its sources to Paschal's *Digest* sections, and the 1925 Penal Code traces back to the Codes of 1856—the Old Code. The abbreviation *O.C.*, used for this purpose without explanation, has baffled many readers.

When recompilation of the statutes into codes was begun, the historical information was placed in notes at the end of the articles, since usually the source article could not be singled out for identification. Modern source references frequently include model acts or uniform laws as well as, or instead of, previous statutes.

A valuable feature of the "Black Statutes" has been the explanatory articles in some of the volumes, in which noted authorities comment on various fields of law.[6] Unfortunately, many of these have been lost to attorneys when a new volume superseded the old one without repeating or replacing the article. Most state and law school libraries keep the superseded volumes, although the individual law office cannot afford space to do so. Hence, loan or photocopy should make them available to any attorney.

Notes

1. A list of these documents is included in the bibliography to Chapter 1.

2. These indexes, compiled by Raines and by Finlay and Simmons, are listed in the bibliography to this chapter.

3. Appropriations acts do not appear in the *Session Law Service*, but are printed in the bound volume.

4. A similar table is given in 1 R. STAYTON, TEXAS FORMS WITH PRACTICE COMMENTARIES § 39 (1957).

5. 6 TEXAS L. REV. 165, 327, 475 (1928).

6. Appendix A gives a list of these articles.

Bibliography

Dallam, James W. *Digest of the Laws of Texas.* Baltimore: Toy, 1845.

Finlay, George P., and D. E. Simmons. *Index to Gammel's Laws of Texas, 1822–1905.* Austin: Gammel, 1906.

Gammel, H. P. N. *Laws of Texas 1822–1897.* 10 vols. Austin, 1898.

Hartley, Oliver C. *Digest of the Laws of Texas.* Philadelphia: Thomas, Cowperthwaite, 1850.

Livingston, Edward. *Complete Works . . . on Criminal Jurisprudence.* 2 vols. New York: National Prison Association of the United States of America, 1873. Reprint, Montclair: Pallvison Smith, 1968.

——. *Projet of the Civil Code of Louisiana of 1825.* New Orleans: T. J. Moran's Sons, 1937.

Oldham, Williamson S., and George W. White. *Digest of the General Statute Laws of the State of Texas.* Austin: Marshall, 1859.

Paschal, George W. *A Digest of the Laws of Texas . . . from 1754 to 1873, carefully annotated.* 4th ed. 2 vols. Washington, D.C.: W. H. and O. H. Morrison, 1874.

Pimsleur, Meira G., ed. *Checklists of Basic American Legal Publications.* South Hackensack, N.J.: Fred B. Rothman Co., 1962–. Section 1: Statutes. Section 2: Session Laws.

Raines, Cadwell W. *Analytical Index to the Laws of Texas, 1823–1905.* Austin: Von Boeckmann-Jones, 1906.

Sayles, John, and Henry Sayles. *Early Laws of Texas, 1731–1879.* 3 vols. Saint Louis: Gilbert, 1888.

Stayton, Robert W. *Texas Forms with Practice Commentaries.* 11 vols. 4th ed. Kansas City: Vernon, 1957-1962.

Texas, Commission to Revise and Digest the Laws. *Report.* Galveston: Galveston News Office, 1879. Also in 6 *Texas L. Rev.* 165, 327, 473 (1927-1928).

Vernon's Annotated Civil and Criminal Statutes of the State of Texas. 26 vols. Kansas City: Vernon, 1926–1927.

Vernon's Sayles' Annotated Civil Statutes of the State of Texas. 5 vols. Kansas City: Vernon, 1914.

West's Texas Statutes and Codes. 5 vols. Saint Paul: West, 1974.

Wilkinson, A. E. *Edward Livingston and the Penal Codes.* 1 *Texas L. Rev.* 25 (1922).

4. Legislative History and Statutory Interpretation

The legislative history of Texas statutes is not as simple a matter as that of congressional acts. However, some extrinsic aids to interpretation do exist, and in general the courts are receptive to their use. General rules of construction are set out in the civil statutes,[1] and the legislature recently adopted a Code Construction Act[2] which is somewhat more specific in enumerating the extrinsic aids that may be used.

The Legislative Reference Library (formerly the Legislative Reference Bureau of the State Library) for many years has endeavored to collect everything possible to aid in the construction of statutes but has met with small success. However, it does have some unpublished reports and studies in addition to the usual state documents. Commercial enterprises can now provide assistance on a current basis and may succeed in maintaining a collection with retrospective value.

A pioneering project in computerization was begun in the Sixty-third Legislature, offering instant and continuous information on legislative action. It has been completely successful. All bills introduced were fed into the computer, which compiled a subject index, an author index, a status account, and a complete history of each bill, with dates of action and the journal page where it is related. A "hot line" gives the citizen access to this information. This project seems to offer hope for a more complete record of legislative history for the future. Debates are taped but not transcribed as yet.

Legislative Journals

House and Senate journals are published daily during a session of the legislature and later appear in bound volumes, indexed. As a rule they do not record floor debate but merely furnish the formal actions taken on bills. For this reason they are of little help in determining legislative intent; but they are not completely devoid of information. Occasionally a floor amendment adding or deleting phrases before passage can provide useful evidence. A governor's message will sometimes indicate the purpose of a bill or the facts leading to its passage. Members of both houses are allowed to state the reasons for their votes, which may be quite useful. Legislative manuals are published for each legislature and furnish clues to what may or may not be found in the journals.

Reports of standing committees have not in the past contained any information and have consisted usually of a mere recommendation that a bill pass or not pass. In some years, however, the rules have required that reports must include reasons for the committee's recommendations, and recently the committees have shown less reluctance to provide such reasons.

When a bill is reported from the committee to the floor for second reading in the house, it must contain a bill analysis. This is usually a section-by-section analysis of the bill's content, not of the reasons for the committee's report. The senate has had no standard procedure; some committees have had analyses made, but they are not printed and distributed with the bills.

Reports of committees are not printed in the journals, but a file of them is kept in the Legislative Reference Library along with the bills. Reports of special investigating committees have at times appeared in the journals, but this procedure is no longer customary.

Bills

Copies of bills may be obtained, during the session and immediately afterward, from the Bill Distribution Room of either house. Commercial services also furnish copies.

The enrolled bill is filed with the secretary of state after being signed by the governor and is the official copy of the law. All bills and all proposed amendments to them are deposited in the Legislative Reference Library, whether or not enacted. The library's collection of bills begins with 1951.

The Governor

The governor's inaugural address usually contains a statement of his legislative program, which may furnish insight into the reason for enactment of a law. This speech, the "State of the State" address, and various emergency messages are printed in the House and Senate journals. Veto messages too may be useful.

Since 1950, press releases issued by the governor's office have been filed in the Legislative Reference Library; they may sometimes be found also in newspaper files. These are a source of information on the governor's reasons for signing or vetoing a bill. Some governors have written to the secretary of state, calling attention to specific problems connected with a bill just signed; these letters are on file with the enrolled bills.

The Legislative Council

The Texas Legislative Council is a permanent interim committee of the legislature, created as a research agency to investigate questions submitted by the legislature. It has the authority to initiate studies itself but rarely does so. Its reports are submitted to the legislature with recommendations for action and are also published for general distribution. These reports are among the most valuable sources of legislative history. Among other duties the council publishes annual reports on the statutory revision program, which it supervises.

The Civil Judicial Council

The annual report of the Civil Judicial Council contains not only useful statistics on the operation of the courts but also, from time to time, recommendations for legislative action. These are usually concerned with the machinery for administration of justice. The council was quite influential in the passage of the act giving rule-making power to the supreme court and in the drafting of the rules promulgated under it.

The Attorney General

Attorney-general opinions are doubly important as sources of information on legislative interpretation. Since an opinion may forestall litigation, it is possibly the highest available, if not the only, authority. In addition, opinions sometimes contain items of legislative history that are unavailable from other sources.

Other aids from the attorney general's office include the published results of studies on law enforcement. These usually comment on inadequacies of existing legislation and therefore may have some bearing on subsequent action. Publication and use of materials concerning the attorney general's office will be more fully discussed in Chapter 8.

Research Agencies

Various independent bodies concern themselves from time to time with research on state government. At the University of Texas, the Institute of Public Affairs (now the Lyndon Baines Johnson School of Public Affairs) and the Bureau of Business Research have conducted some useful investigations. The Institute of Urban Studies at the University of Houston has been particularly active in constitutional-revision studies.

The Texas Research League is a quasi-public organization, financed by contributions from Texas business firms and individuals. It conducts research, analysis, and fact-finding on problems facing the state government, its agencies and departments, and local government entities. Its services are provided without charge to the governmental units receiving them.

Other State Agencies

Most state agencies and departments are required to submit annual reports to the governor or the legislature. These reports, available through depository programs to libraries over the state, frequently supply descriptions of problems that have led to changes in the laws. Anything of a financial nature—recommendations of the Legislative Budget Board, for example—may be helpful if the recommendations were adopted by the legislature.

Subscription Services

Like the nation's capital, state capitals attract many commercial enterprises which furnish information on government activities, and Austin is no exception. For the most part, only current information is provided; organization for permanent retrospective value has been attempted but is yet to be realized.

The Texas Legislative Information Service offers a daily report of activities of the house and senate while the legislature is in session, including the full text of bills introduced. It gives whatever news is released from committee meetings, but no complete reports or hearings. It can also furnish reports on activities of state agencies. Prices vary according to the service desired.

The Executive Information Network (EIN) publishes daily reports on the activities of the legislature and its committees, supplemented by a weekly journal, *Texas in Action*, which includes material on various departments and agencies. It compiles a day-by-day journal of legislative (or constitutional-convention) activities, with capsule accounts of the debate.

The Long News Service publishes various weekly reports on politics and different phases of state government. Confined to newsletter format, these reports are useful for current awareness but of little permanent value.

Notes

1. TEX. REV. CIV. STAT. ANN. art. 10 (1969).
2. *Id.* art. 5429b-2 (supp. 1974).

5. Courts and Court Reports

The Judicial System

The supreme court was established by the Constitution of the Republic, with unlimited and conclusive appellate jurisdiction. Restrictions have been imposed increasingly in successive constitutions, and the court is now subject to a maze of constitutional and statutory limitations, intended to prevent too burdensome a case load. In the historical context, therefore, it is necessary to use caution in the approach to any decision dealing with the court's jurisdiction until contemporary statutes and constitutional provisions have been checked.[1]

Under various constitutions the justices have been sometimes elected and sometimes appointed. Usually these differences are unimportant; but during the period immediately following the Civil War they had some impact on the development of the court. After the United States Congress refused to approve the Texas Constitution of 1866, General Sheridan removed all state officials, including the justices of the supreme court, and substituted his own appointees. The "Military Court" thus appointed lasted until the end of the Reconstruction period. However, since it had no constitutional basis, its decisions are generally considered to have little or no precedential value.[2]

The three justices named under the Constitution of 1869 were still very much a part of the Reconstruction system. In 1874, in an effort to keep this regime undisturbed and maintain the appointive system, the court voided an election which had adopted a constitutional amendment and elected a new court. The decision was made on the basis of a semicolon in the constitutional provision on elections, and the court was promptly dubbed the "Semicolon Court." The decision was ignored, the new justices took office, and for many years all opinions of the Semicolon Court were disparaged by Texas jurists.[3] In modern times they are accepted as precedents, with the exception of the *Semicolon Case* itself.[4]

The 1876 constitution created a court of appeals in addition to a supreme court. The court of appeals was given exclusive jurisdiction in criminal appeals and a very limited civil jurisdiction as well. A few years later the civil docket had grown so heavy that the legislature established a commission of appeals to assist both courts in handling it. The original statute in 1879 provided that cases could be referred to the commission by consent of the parties; in 1881 the two courts also were granted that authority. In 1889 a further amendment gave the supreme court exclusive right to refer cases for decision.

The commission was abolished in 1891, when a constitutional amendment established a court system in which it was unnecessary. The court of appeals was replaced by a court of criminal appeals—the first appellate court in Anglo-American jurisprudence to have exclusively criminal jurisdiction. The courts of civil appeals were created at the same time; their jurisdiction was and is exclusively civil, intermediate in most instances, although final for cases originating in the county and justice courts. Their decisions are appealable to the supreme court by certified question or by writ of error.

In 1918 the legislature again provided a commission of appeals, similar to that of 1879–1891, to lighten the load of the three-judge supreme court. Its opinions were reviewed by the court, and those adopted by the justices were accepted as the equivalent of supreme court opinions. If the court merely approved the holding or issued the recommended judgment, the decisions were of lesser authority. However, it was not always clear from the report just what action the court had taken, and eventually it was decided that all commission opinions accepted by the court should be adopted and published as official.

A similar commission was created in 1925 to aid the court of criminal appeals. The precedential difficulties encountered before were avoided by providing from the beginning that the commission's opinions, when approved by the court, should be equal in authority to those of the court.

In 1945 the supreme court was enlarged to nine members, the commissioners in office at the time being designated as the additional justices. The same action was taken on the criminal side in 1966, the two commissioners being added to the court to provide five judges. However, only a few years later the workload of criminal cases had increased so greatly that it became necessary to re-establish a commission. The number of commissioners is left to the discretion of the presiding judge; at present there are two permanent ones, plus two rotating positions to be held by district judges or retired appellate judges for varying periods.

The system of lower courts is dictated largely by the constitution, but under the authority of the phrase "such other courts as may be provided by law" the legislature has created various kinds of courts needed in different localities. Some, such as corporation courts and special criminal district courts, have only criminal jurisdiction; small claims courts handle civil suits; county courts at law have both civil and criminal jurisdiction. For some counties there are courts of domestic relations and juvenile courts, and even special probate courts, although the county courts have general probate jurisdiction. Since no cases are published from these lower courts, they have little interest for legal research. Even the district courts, which are trial courts of general jurisdiction, do not publish opinions.

A 1972 report from a supreme court task force recommended a reorganization of the judicial branch under a plan which includes merging the two courts of last resort and setting up a greatly simplified system of lower and intermediate courts. The plan for this modified Article V of the constitution was defeated in the Sixty-third Legislature and failed again of adoption in the Constitutional Convention of 1974. It will probably be submitted to the next legislature in the same or a similar version.

Court Reports

The Supreme Court of the Republic decided no cases until 1840, and even then had no official reporter. The decisions for the next six years are collected in Dallam's *Opinions of the Supreme Court of Texas.* Originally these decisions formed the second part of Dallam's *Digest,* already described in Chapter 3. For this reason the first page of the *Opinions* is numbered 357—a fact conducive to misunderstanding. Having no real title of its own, the volume has been bound with many different spine titles: *Dallam's Decisions, Dallam's Opinions, Texas Reports Dallam,* and *Texas Reports 0.*

In 1846 the state appointed court reporters, and the official publication of reports began soon after. The *Texas Reports* formed the only source of supreme court opinions until the appearance of the *Southwestern Reporter* in 1886. The pre-*Southwestern* years are covered by volumes 1-65 of the *Texas Reports,* a total of sixty-six volumes. This anomaly is caused by the existence of a volume known as *25 Texas Supplement,* which contains the decisions of 1860-1861. These opinions were not published until after the Civil War, and the volume was given this designation to keep it in correct chronological order after volume 25. The *Texas Reports* include also the opinions of the two commissions of appeals which were adopted by the supreme court. If the court merely approved the judgment of the commissioners, the cases were not reported officially.

When the court of appeals was created, the state began a separate set of official reports for criminal cases, the *Texas Court of Appeals Reports* (officially entitled *Cases Argued and Adjudged in the Court of Appeals of the State of Texas*). The civil cases before the court were never reported in full, but the four-volume set usually called *White and Willson* (formally entitled *Condensed Reports of Decisions in Civil Cases in the Court of Appeals*) contains abridged versions of the court's opinions.

Cases referred to the commission of appeals by the supreme court were published in the official reports if the opinion was adopted by the court. If the court merely approved the judgment, the case remained unreported; however, after the first few volumes of the *Southwestern Reporter* [5] all of the commission's decisions appeared there. Cases referred by the court of appeals appeared in *White and Willson.* Those referred by consent were published only in obscure and short-lived legal gazettes;[6] but a collection of them was published later as *Posey's Unreported Cases* (S. A. Posey, comp., *Texas Unreported Cases*). Many of those selected by Posey were land cases, and his foreword states that, since they are cases in which both attorneys had strong arguments and expected to win, they are among the most interesting of the period.

After the court of appeals was replaced by the court of criminal appeals, the reports were renamed *Texas Criminal Reports.* The volumes continued the same sequence of numbers, so that the first thirty volumes remain under the old title and the new name begins with volume 31. However, some privately bound sets made the transition at a different volume; so some variation occurs. The early volumes are frequently cited by the newer title. Cases from volume 22 on appear in the *Southwestern Reporter.*

From 1892 to 1911 the state published the *Texas Civil Appeals Reports* (not to be confused with White and Willson's *Civil Cases in the Court of Appeals*). The sixty-two volumes of this set are now ignored, even in citation forms, the *Southwestern Reporter* being the only accepted source. Another unofficial set, the *Texas Court Reporter*, was published briefly at the beginning of the century. Apparently a competitor of the *Southwestern*, it came to an end after twenty volumes. All of the cases in it appear also in the *Southwestern,* so far as can be ascertained.

One other volume of reports must be mentioned, if only because it is still listed as one of those covered by *Shepard's Texas Citations* (see Chapter 7). This is *Robards' Conscript Cases,* a collection of abstracts of supreme court decisions in habeas corpus cases resulting from conscription by the Confederate States' military forces. Understandably, these cases have not been cited since 1866.

Since 1886 almost all appellate cases in Texas courts have been reported in the *Southwestern Reporter.* Before volume 15 it did not publish the civil cases in the court of appeals, and a very few cases in the courts of civil appeals were never published. Commission of appeals opinions not adopted by the supreme court are included, beginning at about volume 12. Since 1963, when the state failed to appropriate funds for official publication of reports, the *Southwestern* has been the only source for Texas cases. However, it has not been declared the official organ of the state, as has been done in some jurisdictions.

In addition to the *Southwestern Reporter,* West publishes the *Texas Cases* as a separate set, with one volume containing the cases from two volumes of the regional reporter. This set has assumed some of the functions of an official publication: the volumes contain memorials to deceased judges, amendments to the Rules of Civil Procedure, and similar items. The Texas Edition of the *Southwestern* advance sheets supplies writ-of-error information.

Very occasionally it happens that the court withdraws an opinion that has been published in the advance sheets, replacing it with another. The second opinion necessarily appears at a different page, and sometimes even in a later volume. If it has been cited anywhere with the original page reference, the correction may or may not be noted; if not, confusion is inevitable.

Since published cases are at least several weeks old when they appear in advance sheets, the need for prompt information has given rise to various independent publications which emphasize fast service rather than permanent format. The *Texas Supreme Court Journal* gives supreme court opinions in full, as well as lists of cases docketed, disposition of petitions for writ of error, and other proceedings of the court. A useful feature is the section that gives the points on which a writ was granted or refused. The *Journal* ordinarily reaches the lawyer on Saturday after decisions are handed down on Wednesday.[7] There is no cumulation, and the cases are not indexed; the date of the decision is the only clue to location.

The *Texas Syllabi* originally contained synopses of both supreme court and criminal appeals decisions but is now confined to supreme court opinions alone. It is mimeographed and mailed out on Wednesday night, thus reaching subscribers earlier than does the printed *Journal*. It gives much the same information except that it supplies only an abstract of the opinions. This synopsis is a very detailed one, however, not a mere digest paragraph, and is done by an experienced and skillful writer.

Copies of criminal appeals opinions are available on an informal subscription basis from court personnel, as are some of the civil appeals opinions. Usually someone in the clerk's office undertakes this service. Criminal appeals opinions are abstracted in the attorney general's monthly *Crime Prevention Newsletter*.

The State Bar publishes the *Texas Lawyers' Weekly Digest* (formerly *Texas Lawyers' Weekly Letter*), giving very brief informal digests of decisions in all state appellate courts, all federal appellate cases originating in Texas, and selected federal district court opinions. It also notes Texas attorney-general opinions. As a related service, the bar will furnish copies of any opinion abstracted, at a reasonable price. Semiannual indexes are published and are very helpful in locating cases not yet included in the cumulative tables of cases published in the *Texas Digest* (see Chapter 10).

Summary

TEXAS SUPREME COURT

1836–1840 (Republic)	No cases decided.
1840–1844 (Republic)	*Dallam's Decisions,* 1 vol.
1846–1886	*Texas Reports* 1-65.
1886–1963	*Texas Reports* 66–163 and *Southwestern Reporter.*
1963–	*Southwestern* only.

COURT OF APPEALS

1876–1891	*Texas Court of Appeals Reports* 1–30; after 1886, *Southwestern* also (criminal cases). *White and Willson*, 4 vols. (civil cases).

COMMISSION OF APPEALS

1879–1891	*Texas Reports* (adopted by supreme court); *White and Willson* (cases referred by court of

	appeals); *Posey's Unreported Cases* (cases referred by consent); after 1886, *Southwestern*.
COMMISSION OF APPEALS (second)	
1918–1934	*Texas Reports* and *Southwestern*, if adopted by Supreme Court; *Southwestern* only, if merely approved.
1934–1945	*Texas Reports* and *Southwestern* in all cases, since all were adopted.
COURTS OF CIVIL APPEALS	
1892–1911	*Texas Civil Appeals Reports*, 62 vols., and *Southwestern*.
1911–	*Southwestern* only.
COURT OF CRIMINAL APPEALS	
1892–1963	*Texas Criminal Reports* 31–172 and *Southwestern*.
1963–	*Southwestern* only.

Notes

1. At least once the supreme court has assumed jurisdiction in somewhat unorthodox fashion. *See* In re House Bill 537, 256 S.W. 573 (1923), where the court passed on the constitutionality

of a statute without having an actual case or controversy before it. The law directed the court to assume a duty which the court believed was outside its constitutional power.

2. For the Military Court's decisions, see *Texas Reports*, vol. 30, p. 375, to vol. 33, p. 583.

3. For the Semicolon Court's decisions, see *Texas Reports*, vol. 33, p. 585, to vol. 39.

4. Ex parte Rodríguez, 39 Tex. 705 (1874).

5. Usually cited thus, although the title page gives *South Western Reporter*.

6. *Texas Law Journal* (Austin), 6 vols., 1882-1896; *Texas Law Journal* (Tyler), 5 vols., 1887-1892; *Texas Law Reporter* (Austin), 3 vols., 1882-1896; *Texas Law Review* (Austin), 6 vols., 1883-1886.

7. A predecessor, the *Texas Supreme Court Reporter*, published similar information until 1956.

Bibliography

Butte, George C. *Early Development of Law and Equity in Texas.* 26 *Yale L.J.* 699 (1917).

Carter, Keith. *The Texas Court of Criminal Appeals*. Ph.D. thesis, Columbia University, 1932; reprinted in 11 *Texas L. Rev.* 1, 185, 301, 455 (1932-1933).

Cases Argued and Adjudged in the Court of Appeals of the State of Texas. 30 vols. Published by the State of Texas, 1877-1892. Imprint varies.

Gilmer, Daffan. *Early Courts and Lawyers of Texas.* 12 *Texas L. Rev.* 435 (1934).

Hall, Ford W. *Adoption of the Common Law by Texas.* 28 *Texas L. Rev.* 801 (1950).

Hart, James. *Appellate Jurisdiction of the Supreme Court of Texas.* 29 *Texas L. Rev.* 285 (1951).

McKnight, Joseph W. *Spanish Influence on the Texas Law of Civil Procedure.* 39 *Texas L. Rev.* 24 (1959).

Markham, Edward L. *Reception of the Common Law of England in Texas and the Judicial Attitude toward That Reception, 1840-1859.* 29 *Texas L. Rev.* 904 (1952).

Norvell, James. *Oran M. Roberts and the Semicolon Court.* 37 *Texas L. Rev.* 279 (1959).

Posey, S. A., comp. *Texas Unreported Cases.* 2 vols. Saint Louis: Gilbert, 1886-1891.

Sales, James B., and John W. Cliff. *Jurisdiction in the Texas Supreme Court and Courts of Civil Appeals.* 26 *Baylor L. Rev.* 501 (1974).

South Western Reporter. 300 vols. Saint Paul: West, 1887-1928. Second Series, vols. 1-, 1928-.

Texas Cases Reported in the South Western Reporter. 300 vols. in 97 books. Saint Paul: West, 1887-1928. Second Series, vols. 1-, 1928-.

Texas Court Reporter. 20 vols. Austin: Ben C. Jones Co., 1900-1908.

Texas Criminal Reports: Cases Determined in the Court of Criminal Appeals. Vols. 31-172. Published by the State of Texas, 1893-1963. Imprint varies.

Texas Lawyers' Weekly Digest (formerly *Texas Lawyers' Weekly Letter*). Austin: State Bar of Texas, 1964-.

Texas Reports: Cases Adjudged in the Supreme Court. 164 vols. (vols. 1-163, plus vol. 25 Texas Supplement). Published by the State of Texas, 1846-1963. Imprint varies.

Texas Supreme Court Journal. Austin, 1957-.

Texas Supreme Court Reporter. 28 vols. Austin, 1932-1957.

Texas Syllabi. Austin, 1928-.

Wharton, Clarence. *Early Judicial History of Texas.* 12 *Texas L. Rev.* 311 (1934).

White, John P., and Sam A. Willson, comps. *Condensed Reports of Decisions in Civil Cases in the Court of Appeals.* 4 vols. Saint Louis: Gilbert, 1883-1892. Vols. 2-4 were compiled by Willson without White's collaboration, but the entire set is known as *White and Willson.*

Wynn, Leila. *History of the Civil Courts of Texas.* 60 *S.W. Hist. Q.* 1 (1956).

6. Court Rules and Procedure

The 1836 constitution required that Congress should introduce the common law of England but added, "with such modifications as our circumstances require." Later Congresses and legislatures took full advantage of this clause, adopting laws on community property, homestead exemption, conveyancing, and intestate succession which were certainly inspired by Spanish precedents rather than by common law. For rules of pleading and practice, the entire common law system was rejected in favor of pleading "by petition and answer."[1] The Field Codes, so influential in many other parts of the country, had little effect in Texas, where the drafters preferred to rely on Livingston's work.

One innovation of the early years, since adopted in other jurisdictions, was the fusing of law and equity into one form of action. An 1840 act provided for this union;[2] as one court commented, it instructed the judge to try all cases at law, and if he could not succeed in that he was to "ascend the woolsack and chancel it."[3]

All early constitutions provided that the supreme court should have the power to prescribe rules of procedure; but until 1876 a clause was always added that the power should be exercised in a manner consistent with the laws. As a result, a long tradition of procedural statutes was established, beginning in 1840 with the same act that rejected common law pleading. Even when the 1876 constitution omitted the usual proviso, the court adopted only a few short rules. Tradition was later restored by constitutional amendment.

The few rules promulgated by the court during the century of statutory control dealt for the most part with the conduct of the court's business or merely repeated the language of the statutes. The original version of the rules for the supreme court and the district courts appears in volume 1 of the *Texas Reports,* and amendments are contained in many of the subsequent volumes.[4] After the creation of the courts of civil appeals, their rules were included. Rules for the court of appeals were published in its *Reports,* in volumes 2 and 27; volume 31 printed rules for the new court of criminal appeals, but the subsequent amendments were not so published.

In 1939 a long-standing dissatisfaction with statutory rules of procedure culminated in a campaign which induced the legislature to authorize the supreme court to promulgate rules of civil procedure for the trial courts of the state. The legislators reserved the right to reject the drafted rules, but in fact this power has never been exercised. Although influenced to some extent by the Federal Rules of Civil Procedure, the rules adopted in 1941 retained the individual features of Texas practice. They have been amended often but are still in force. Amendments are printed in the Texas edition of the *Southwestern* advance sheets and in the bound volumes of *Texas Cases*; annual pamphlet editions of the rules are available from West, and the Black Statutes contain a six-volume set of annotated Rules of Civil Procedure.

The statutes regulating criminal procedure were first codified in the Old Code of 1856, and the tradition of statutory control has lasted through four general revisions of the laws and the 1965 Code of Criminal Procedure. There seems to be no movement in favor of court-promulgated rules in this field.

Three peculiarities of Texas procedure may present difficulties for an out-of-state attorney. Venue requirements are both complex and stringent; however, case annotations are available in almost bewildering profusion. All civil cases are submitted to the jury on special issues, which may amount to well over a hundred minutely detailed questions in a complicated case. Hodges' classic monograph on this subject is listed in the bibliography. The third unfamiliar area is that of title to land, where all actions are in the form of "trespass to try title," an action adopted by the Congress of the Republic in 1840[5] as a substitute for common law ejectment. All these topics are covered by statutes and rules of procedure, and reasonably complete surveys may be found in *Texas Jurisprudence Second.* McDonald's standard treatise on Texas civil procedure, also listed in the bibliography, will provide more precise and scholarly treatment, and annotations to the statutes furnish full reference to law review articles on each topic. The historical notes are also of value.

Notes

1. Tex. Laws 1840: An Act To Regulate the Proceedings in Civil Suits. 2 H. GAMMEL, LAWS OF TEXAS 262 (1898).
2. Ibid.
3. Whiting v. Turley, Dallam 435 (Tex. 1842).
4. The original editions carried this material, but it was frequently omitted from reprints.
5. Tex. Laws 1840: An Act To Provide the Mode of Trying Titles to Lands. 2 H. GAMMEL, LAWS OF TEXAS 310 (1898).

Bibliography

Clark, Allen. *Venue in Civil Actions in Texas.* Saint Louis: Thomas, 1953.

Franki, Julius. *The Change from Legislative to Court Control of Procedure in Civil Actions. Tex. R. Civ. Proc. Ann.* xxvii (1942).

Hodges, Gus M. *Special Issue Submission in Texas.* Austin: University of Texas Law School Foundation, 1959; supp., 1969.

McDonald, Roy W. *Texas Civil Practice in District and County Courts.* 4 vols. Mundelein, Ill.: Callaghan, 1950. Replacement volumes, 1965–1971.

State Bar of Texas. *Pattern Jury Instructions.* 2 vols. Austin, 1970.

Stayton, Robert W. *Methods of Practice in Texas Courts.* Kansas City: Vernon, 1935.

Texas Civil Judicial Council. *Local Rules of the District Courts of Texas*. [Austin], 1974.

7. Citators and Writ Tables

An appellate case may reach the supreme court by one of three routes. A *direct appeal* is possible from a district or county court decision denying or granting an injunction, where the constitutionality of a statute or the validity of the order forms the basis of the appeal. A court of civil appeals may *certify a question* of law if its decision is (*a*) final, and (*b*) of wide application and importance. Most cases come to the court by *petition for writ of error*, filed in the court of civil appeals in which the intermediate appeal was heard. Writ may be granted on a question of law, for good cause; this might be a strong dissent, conflict in decisions between the courts of civil appeals, or a question important to the state, such as the construction of a statute. The court customarily dismisses a certified question if writ jurisdiction exists.

It must be noted that, in addition to the statute defining the positive writ jurisdiction of the court,[1] another statute places restrictions on it.[2] For example, writ of error may not be granted in a slander case or a divorce, even if the other qualifications are met. The several provisions of each statute must be checked to be sure that jurisdiction exists.

As of 1975, the court may take one of four actions on the writ: it may be granted, refused, refused no reversible error (n.r.e.), or dismissed, this last being either by agreement of the parties or by action of the court.[3] If writ is refused, the authority of the case is strengthened, since the court has said in effect that the question of law was correctly decided in the intermediate court. The n.r.e. notation indicates that the court is not convinced that the opinion below has stated the law correctly in all respects; determination of the precedential value of the opinion is complicated by several factors. A further consideration is that the significance of the notations has varied from time to time.[4] Evaluation of the writ history of a case is essential for the attorney, but it is far from easy.

The *Texas Writs of Error Table,* published by West as an adjunct to the *Southwestern Reporter,* serves as a special kind of citator for Civil Appeals cases, and is an indispensable tool for the Texas lawyer. It gives the original action on the writ petition, any later action that supersedes it, and the citation for any court opinion in its later history. Thus, although a refusal or n.r.e. is usually a permanent notation, it may be replaced by a United States Supreme Court opinion; "granted" is replaced either by "dismissed" or by the citation of the final opinion in the case. Very occasionally the court writes an opinion in refusing the writ; in this case the citation of course replaces the refusal. Mandamus action also is noted.

New editions of the *Table* are issued at intervals, and in the interim it is kept up to date by supplements printed on pink pages in the Texas edition of the *Southwestern* advance sheets. These pages should always be checked, in addition to the *Table* itself, even for quite old cases; the span covered by any one such supplement may be over 150 volumes of *Southwestern.* The coverage of the *Table* starts with volume 20, the first in which civil appeals cases appear.

Shepard's Southwestern Reporter Citations resembles other regional citators in coverage, with citations in all units of the National Reporter System, all reporters for United States Supreme Court cases, and the annotated reports. It adds to these the information for Texas writs of error, but up to volume 306 of *Southwestern Second* it merely marks with an asterisk the cases affected by writs; after that time the specific disposal of the writ is given.

A new edition of *Shepard's Texas Citations* appeared in 1974. It also furnishes writ information, but the transition from simple asterisk to specific writ history takes place at volume 256 *South-*

western Reporter, thus adding considerable coverage to that of the other set.

As was true of previous editions, citations to the early volumes of all official Texas court reports are given in usual form; but after the cases began appearing in the first volume of the *Southwestern Reporter,* only a cross reference to *Southwestern* is found under the official citation. The user must then turn to another section of the volume, where the information usually included in state citators is given under the parallel *Southwestern* citation. This transition is a little confusing, although routine for Texas attorneys; but in the new edition confusion is compounded by placing this section for early official reports at the beginning of the second volume of the set, completely out of chronological order.

Like other state citators, this one includes references to law reviews of national scope as well as those published within the state and emphasizing local coverage. The beginning date for such citations varies widely. Current paper supplements have added citations to the ALI *Restatements,* with retrospective coverage back to their first publication dates.

The statute edition adds to the normal coverage of such sections citations to *Branch's Annotated Penal Code,* a set widely used by Texas lawyers. A very recent innovation is the addition of citations to *Texas Pattern Jury Charges,* a publication of the State Bar. As yet there are no references to Texas attorney-general opinions, but the trend toward uniformity in the Shepard publications indicates that this too may soon be added.

King's Conflicting Cases, occasionally mentioned in publications dating from the early years of this century, was a three-volume set designed to be a kind of citator. It was not continued after 1911.

The following table, from Simpson, *Notations on Applications for Writs of Error,* is reprinted, with permission, from the December 1949 *Texas Bar Journal,* vol. 12, no. 11.

Texas Cases

Table of Notations Used on Applications for Writs of Error

Notation	Date[a]	Statute or Rule Defining Notation
Refused [writ ref'd]	Sept. 1, 1892 to June 14, 1927	None. Cf. Acts 1892, 1st C. S., Ch. 14, p. 20; Art. 943, R. S. 1895; Art. 1544, R. S. 1911; Art. 1746, R. S. 1925.
	June 14, 1927 to present	Acts 1927, Reg. Sess., ch. 144, p. 214, amending Art. 1728, R. S. 1925; Rule 483, Texas Rules of Civil Procedure.
Refused for Want of Merit; Ref. Want Merit; Ref. W.M. [writ ref'd w.o.m.]	Sept. 1, 1941 to Feb. 1, 1946	Rule 483, Texas Rules of Civil Procedure.
Refused, No Reversible Error; Ref. N.R.E. [writ ref'd n.r.e.]	Feb. 1, 1946 to present	Rule 483, Texas Rules of Civil Procedure.
Dismissed; Dismissed for Want of Jurisdiction; Dismissed WOJ [writ dism'd w.o.j.]	Sept. 1, 1892 to July 1, 1917[b]	None. Cf. Acts of 1892, 1st C. S., ch. 15, § 5, p. 26; Art. 996, R. S. 1895; Art. 1591, R. S. 1911; Acts 1892,

[a]Date of Supreme Court's action on the application. See tables of cases reviewed, published in the Texas Reports, for exact date of action.

Meaning

Supreme Court approved result reached by C.C.A. but did not necessarily approve opinion. Brackenridge v. Cobb, 85 Tex. 448, 21 S.W. 1034; Fleming v. Texas Loan Agency, 87 Tex. 238, 27 S.W. 126. Refusal might not even mean approval of result reached, where error was not preserved and presented to Supreme Court. See Terrell v. Middleton, 108 Tex. 14, 17, 191 S.W. 1138, 1139; City of San Angelo v. Deutsch, 126 Tex. 532, 540, 91 S.W. 2d 308, 312.

Judgment of C.C.A. correct and principles of law declared in opinion correctly determined. Hamilton v. Empire Gas & Fuel Co., 134 Tex. 377, 383, 110 S.W. 2d 561, 565; Ohler v. Trinity Portland Cement Co., Tex. Civ. App., 181 S.W. 2d 120, 123.

Judgment of C.C.A. correct but Supreme Court not satisfied that opinion in all respects has correctly declared the law.

Supreme Court not satisfied that opinion of C.C.A. in all respects has correctly declared the law, but is of the opinion that the application presents no error which requires reversal.

Lack of jurisdiction in Supreme Court to consider application. Examples: jurisdiction final in C.C.A., Burnett v. Powell, 86 Tex. 382, 24 S.W. 788, 25 S.W. 17 (boundary suit), Gulf, C. & S. F. R. Co. v. Buford, 85 Tex. 430, 21 S.W. 678 (amount in controversy), Meade v. Leon & H. Blum Land Co., 85 Tex. 513, 22 S.W. 514 (question of fact); defective application, Homes v.

[b]The 1917 act provided that it should become effective on July 1, 1917, but that it should not affect business before the Supreme Court at that time. Records in the clerk's office indicate that applications filed after July 1, 1917, were not acted on by the Supreme Court until after January 1, 1919.

			1st C. S. ch. 14, p. 20; Art. 940, R. S. 1895; Art. 1521, R. S. 1911, and amending acts.
		July 1, 1917[b] to June 14, 1927	Cf. Art. 1591, R. S. 1911, and Acts 1917, Reg. Sess., ch. 75, p. 141, amending Art. 1521, R. S. 1911; Arts. 1728 and 1821, R. S. 1925.
		June 14, 1927 to March 1, 1939	Acts 1927, ch. 144, p. 214, amending Art. 1728, R. S. 1925; Art. 1821, R. S. 1925.
		March 1, 1939 to present	Supreme Court Rule 5a, 131 Tex. v; Rule 483, Texas Rules of Civil Procedure.
	Dismissed for Want of Jurisdiction—Correct Judgment; Dismissed, WOJ—Correct Judgment; Dism. Judgm. Cor. [writ dism'd jdgmt cor.].	March 1, 1939 to Sept. 1, 1941	Supreme Court Rule 5a, 131 Tex. v.

City of Henrietta, 91 Tex. 318. 42 S.W. 1052; application filed too late, Schleicher v. Runge, 90 Tex. 456, 39 S.W. 279; subject matter of controversy has ceased to exist, Robinson v. State, 87 Tex. 562, 29 S.W. 649; judgment of C.C.A. not one which "practically settles the case," Gulf, C. & S. F. R. Co. v. Riordan, 85 Tex. 511, 22 S.W. 514 (1892-1913).

Same as above, except extended to include cases otherwise within jurisdiction of Supreme Court where error committed, if any, was not "of such importance to the jurisprudence of the State as in the opinion of the Supreme Court required correction." Decker v. Kerlicks, 110 Tex. 90, 95, 216 S.W. 385, 386; National Compress Co. v. Hamlin, 114 Tex. 375, 385, 269 S.W. 1024, 1028.

(1) Lack of jurisdiction in Supreme Court to consider application. See examples above. (2) In cases within jurisdiction of Supreme Court, judgment correct but Supreme Court not satisfied that opinion of C.C.A. in all respects has correctly declared the law. Bain Peanut Co. of Texas v. Pinson & Guyer, 119 Tex. 572, 574, 34 S.W. 2d 1090, 1091. (Cf. "Refused" prior to 1927.)

Lack of jurisdiction in Supreme Court to consider application. See examples above. Wood v. Bankers Life & Loan Ass'n of Dallas, 132 Tex. 505, 125 S.W. 2d 262.

In cases within jurisdiction of Supreme Court, judgment correct but Supreme Court not satisfied that opinion of C.C.A in all respects has correctly declared the law. Republic Ins. Co. v. Highland Park Ind. Sch. Dist., 133 Tex. 545, 125 S.W. 2d 270.

Notes

1. TEX. REV. CIV. STAT. ANN. art. 1728 (1962).

2. *Id.* art. 1821 (1964).

3. For complete discussion see the articles cited in the bibliography.

4. See the "Table of Notations Used on Applications for Writs of Error" at the end of this chapter.

Bibliography

Branch's Annotated Penal Code of Texas. 2d ed. 5 vols. Rochester: Lawyers Co-operative Publishing Co., 1956. 3d ed. in progress. San Francisco: Bancroft-Whitney, 1974–.

Calvert, Robert W. *No Evidence and Insufficient Evidence Points of Error*. 38 *Texas L. Rev.* 359 (1960).

——. *Some Problems of Supreme Court Review*. 21 *Texas Bar J.* 75 (1958).

Hart, James P. *Appellate Jurisdiction of the Supreme Court of Texas*. 29 *Texas L. Rev.* 285 (1951).

King, William W., comp. *Conflicting Civil Cases in the Texas Reports*. 3 vols. Saint Louis: Gilbert, 1890.

Restatement in the Courts, The. Unnumbered volumes. Philadelphia: American Law Institute, 1948–.

Shepard's Southwestern Reporter Citations. 3d ed. 2 vols. Colorado Springs: Shepard's Citations, 1950–1971. Supplements.

Shepard's Texas Citations. 5th ed. 3 vols. Colorado Springs: Shepard's Citations, 1974. Supplements.

Simpson, Gordon. *Notations on Applications for Writs of Error*. 12 *Texas Bar J.* 547 (1949).

Texas Pattern Jury Charges. 2 vols. Austin: State Bar of Texas, 1969–1970.

Wilson, Frank M. *Hints on Precedent Evaluation.* 24 *Texas Bar J.* 1037 (1961).

8. Executive Branch

Although it has been said that no one really knows how many boards and agencies are comprised by the executive branch of Texas government, the number certainly approaches two hundred. Some of them exist in name only, having outlived their original purpose. Many are composed wholly or in part of ex officio members, a few are elected, and over a hundred are appointed by the governor. There is no provision for codification of their regulations or even for systematic publication. Most of them make available, on request, copies of rules and regulations; some publish pamphlet editions of pertinent laws. All agencies are supposed to furnish copies of their publications to the State Library for distribution to libraries over the state; some of them, however, do not consider their regulations to be such publications as are meant by the law, and fail to do so. The attorney or scholar who depends on library collections rather than on the agency itself will find it difficult to verify that his sources are up to date.

A reasonably comprehensive account of this branch of government is provided in successive editions of the *Guide to Texas State Agencies*, first published by the Institute of Public Affairs at the University of Texas. It offers information on the origin and functions of each agency, complete with statutory references and tables indicating interrelationships; statements of the qualifications and method of selection of officials are also given. An article in the *Baylor Law Review* some years ago repeated much of this material and added the procedures for practice before the agencies and for appealing their decisions. A great deal of this information is still valid.

The Governor

In contrast to the powerful position of the lieutenant governor as presiding officer of the senate, the governor has had very little actual power up to recent times. He has always had great political influence but traditionally has been regarded as "first among equals" rather than as the head of a strong administrative organization. To some extent this situation has changed. The governor represents the state in its relationship with the federal government and its agencies which dispense funds for state projects. He is also the planning officer designated by the legislature to coordinate the activities of individual agencies for many purposes.

There are various arms of the governor's office, many of which publish reports from time to time. The Department of Intergovernmental Relations, the Criminal Justice Council, the Interagency Natural Resources Council, and several others have regular publications programs.

Attorney General

Although the attorney general is considered for some purposes as a part of the judicial branch, some of his activities are more closely related to the executive. He is charged by the constitution with the duty of giving advice to state and county officials; the legislature has designated many specific agencies and officers who may request such advice, and any others are prohibited from doing so. Even officials of federal agencies must obtain advice through the appropriate Texas officials, as must agencies of other states.

These advisory opinions have taken different forms under different administrations. Frequently an oral opinion is given, which may refer the questioner to some previous published opinion. A memorandum opinion may be issued, signed by an assistant rather than by the attorney general himself. Letter opinions constitute legal advice without the full formality of an official opinion. And, finally, the formal conference opinion may be needed. It resembles an appellate court decision, containing a résumé of the facts, a review of authorities, a statement of the reasoning, and the conclusion reached. It is signed by the attorney general, his top aides, and the full Opinions Committee.

Early opinions are numbered erratically or not at all and are identified by date, person to whom addressed, and sometimes volume and page of reports. Some of them were published in annual reports; some never appeared in print. Beginning in 1939 they were numbered in sequence, prefixed with the letter O; for example, O-235. In 1947 the prefix letter was changed to V; tradition says that the letter was in honor of Victory. This custom endured until 1953, since which time the prefix has been the initial letter of the attorney general's name. Thus, Attorney General Hill's opinions are numbered from H-1, with separate number sequences for his letter advisories (LA), constitutional convention advisories, and open records advisories (OR).

Attorney-general opinions are not binding law, but Texas courts have held repeatedly that they are very persuasive.[1] As was said in Chapter 4, an opinion which forestalls litigation may well be the highest available authority on statutory interpretation. If an agency has followed an opinion for some time without legislative action to the contrary, its authority is naturally strengthened. In any case, an official who has relied on an opinion is protected from liability for any of his actions under its authority. The attorney general's advice is indispensable in filling the gaps left by lack of administrative organization in the state.

In all probability the only complete file extant is that in the attorney general's office.[2] Until the present administration there has been no regular subscription for the opinions, although copies of any one could be obtained on request. Subscriptions are now available, but a fairly high price is charged. Monthly digests have been published since 1947, and a cumulated annual index to them is furnished. An index covering the years 1947–1970 is available, but the opinions before 1947 are indexed only in the office files.

Opinions are noted in the *Texas Lawyers' Weekly Digest* and are included in the annotations to the Black Statutes. Up to the present, they are not covered by *Shepard's Texas Citations.* Some professional associations have indexed the opinions pertinent to their interests, but these are not available to the public.

The attorney general represents the state in civil actions,[3] determining the position of the state on litigated issues according to his interpretation of the law. He may from time to time employ outside counsel to brief or argue questions requiring particular expertise. The briefs in these cases, involving such questions as state boundaries, water rights, or ownership of coastal mineral lands, are valuable sources on the law in these areas and are important to historians as well. They are usually available in state archives, in the files of the courts, and in university libraries.

Miscellaneous publications of the attorney general's office include drafting manuals, citation form guides, and occasional reports of conferences on such subjects as law enforcement and eminent domain. Special reports are issued when occasion demands: for example, a report on the assassination of President Kennedy. The Crime Prevention Division publishes a *Crime Prevention Newsletter*, which is distributed to law-enforcement agencies over the state to keep them up to date on significant cases and attorney-general opinions.

Railroad Commission

The more or less accidental assignment of oil and gas conservation to the jurisdiction of the Railroad Commission has made it one of the most active and important of the state agencies. Regulation of motor carriers occupies a part of its attention, but in general its duties in the field of transportation have been overshadowed by its control of petroleum production.

The commission publishes a vast number of orders and regulations for the various oil fields in the state, but the lack of organization and indexing makes them difficult to use. Two Austin firms furnish information in more accessible form. The State House Reporter offers both daily information and annual summaries, while R. W. Byram Company specializes in practice aids and looseleaf service on regulations.

General Land Office

Created in 1836 to dispose of public lands and to keep records of grants, the land office at present is charged with management of all oil and mineral leases on state-owned lands as well. It also administers a loan program for veterans, enabling them to purchase land. At various times it has published volumes of abstracts and claims and histories of public lands. Recently the commissioner who heads the GLO has added an interest in land use planning and coastal resources to projects of longer standing.

A historical curiosity, of little current value, was the Texas Court of Claims. It was organized in 1856 to investigate claims to Mexican land grants, headrights, bounties, and other claims against the government. It was abolished four years later, its functions being divided between the land office and the comptroller.

Interstate Compacts

Texas has joined with other states for mutual assistance and joint action on some twenty of the many interstate compacts now in effect. The compacts are set out in the statutes, and complete references may be found in the *Guide to Texas State Agencies*. The annual reports of the various commissions which administer the compacts furnish further information. Some, like the Interstate Oil Compact, have rather ambitious publications programs of their own. The Council of State Governments, which sponsors the compacts, offers information on them in the *Book of the States* annual.

Notes

1. Dickson, *Vital Crucible of the Law: Politics and Procedures of the Advisory Opinion Function of the Texas Attorney General*. 9 HOUS. L. REV. 495, 522 (1972).

2. A possible exception is the microfilm edition recently completed at Temple University.

3. The state's attorney, appointed by the court of criminal appeals but independent of it, represents the state in all criminal

cases before the federal courts and in state appellate actions where there is no prosecuting attorney already acting for the state.

Bibliography

Administrative Government in Texas. 47 *Texas L. Rev.* 805 (1969).

Book of the States. Chicago: Council of State Governments, annual.

Burdine, Alton, and Thomas M. Reavley. *Toward a More Effective Administration.* 35 *Texas L. Rev.* 939 (1957).

Guide to Texas State Agencies. 4th ed. Austin: Lyndon Baines Johnson School of Public Affairs, 1973.

Lipscomb, Abner E. *Judicial Control of Administrative Action in Texas.* Waco: Baylor University, 1938. *Baylor Bulletin*, law number, vol. 41, no. 3.

Reavley, Thomas M. *Substantial Evidence and Insubstantial Review: Trial de novo in Texas.* 23 *S.W.L.J.* 239 (1969).

Shepperd, John Ben. *Texas Administrative Procedure for the Practicing Attorney.* 8 *Baylor L. Rev.* 385 (1957).

Texas Civil Judicial Council. *Administrative Procedure Laws in the United States, a Comparative Study.* Austin, 1957.

Texas Legislature, Joint Committee on Organization and Economy. *Government of the State of Texas.* 13 parts. Austin, 1933. The Griffenhagen Report, authorized by H. Con. Res. 58, 41st Legislature.

Governor

Davis, James W. *There Shall Also Be a Lieutenant Governor.* Austin: Institute of Public Affairs, 1967.

Gantt, Fred, Jr. *The Chief Executive in Texas: A Study in Gu-*

bernatorial Leadership. Austin: University of Texas Press, 1964.

Attorney General

Activities of the Attorney General's Office: A Report to the Legislature. Austin. Irregular.
Checklist of Basic American Legal Publications. South Hackensack, N.J.: Fred B. Rothman and Co. Looseleaf 1962–. Section 3: Attorneys General Opinions and Reports.
National Association of Attorneys General. *Report on the Office of Attorney General*. Lexington, Ky., 1971.
Shepperd, John Ben. *Common Law Powers and Duties of the Attorney General*. 7 *Baylor L. Rev.* 1 (1956).
Twenty-four Year Index to the Opinions of the Attorney General of Texas. Dallas: Astro, 1971.

Railroad Commission

Byram, R. W., and Company. *Texas Oil and Gas Handbook: Procedures and Forms*. Rev. ed. Austin, 1970.
Greenhill, Joe, and Robert C. McGinnis. *Practice and Procedure in Oil and Gas Hearings*. 18 *S.W.L.J.* 406 (1964).
MER (Maximum Efficient Recovery) Hearings of the Texas Railroad Commission: Summaries. Austin: State House Reporter, annual.
Peden, Brooks. *Oil and Gas Hearing Aid: Evidence, Procedure and Practice*. Rev. ed. Austin: Byram, 1971.
Rules and Regulations of the Texas Railroad Commission: Oil and Gas. 12 vols. Looseleaf. Austin: Byram, 1937–.
Secondary Recovery Hearings of the Texas Railroad Commission: Summaries. Austin: State House Reporter, annual.
Texas Railroad Commission. *Survey of Secondary Recovery and*

Pressure Maintenance Operations in Texas. Austin: Railroad Commission, annual.

Texas Research League. *The Texas Railroad Commission*. Austin, 1963.

General Land Office

Bishop, Curtis. *Lots of Land*. Austin: Steck, 1943.

Burlage, John. *Abstract of Valid Land Claims in the General Land Office and the Court of Claims*. Austin: Marshall, 1859. Reprint, Austin: Pemberton Press, n.d.

Giles, Bascom. *Handling of the Public Domain: History and Disposition of Texas Public Lands*. Austin: General Land Office, 1940.

Hazel, G. G. *Public Land Law of Texas*. Austin: Gammel, 1938.

Lang, Alden S. *Financial History of the Public Lands in Texas*. Waco: Baylor University, 1932. *Baylor Bulletin* 35, no. 3.

Miller, Thomas Lloyd. *Bounty and Donation Land Grants of Texas, 1835–1888*. Austin: University of Texas Press, 1967.

——. *Public Lands of Texas 1519–1970*. Norman: University of Oklahoma Press, 1970.

Rogan, Octavia. *Land Commissioner Rogan and the Mineral Classification of Texas Public School Lands*. Austin: San Felipe Press, 1968.

Texas, General Land Office. *Abstract of All Original Texas Land Titles* . . . Austin, 1941–1942. 8 vols. Supplements to date.

Texas, General Land Office. *History of Texas Land*. Austin, 1961.

9. State Bar

The Texas Bar Association was organized in 1882 and published its proceedings in annual volumes for the next forty years. From 1923 to 1938 the proceedings appeared in special numbers of the *Texas Law Review*, published in October of each year. These issues are not paged consecutively with the regular volumes of the *Law Review* and usually are not bound with them.

The papers and addresses presented at bar meetings are of considerable interest as commentaries on the development of the law during the period, and the memorials to deceased members offer useful biographical material. After 1938, however, there has been no publication of the complete proceedings.

The passage of the State Bar Act[1] in 1938 effected the integration of the bar, which has been known since that time as the State Bar of Texas. The *Texas Bar Journal* is the organ of the bar; it publishes excellent practice aids, articles on current topics, and information on bar activities. It also continues the practice of printing memorials, although they are now merely brief biographical sketches instead of the sonorous eulogies formerly customary. A cumulative index to the *Journal* was published in 1963 but has not been supplemented.

It was formerly the custom to insert in the *Bar Journal*, from time to time, information on minimum fee schedules, interpretations of the Rules and Canons of Ethics, and similar matters of interest to bar members. These leaflets were designed to be inserted in a binder as a kind of desk book. This practice has been discontinued; the opinions on ethics are published in the

Journal as they are issued, and the State Bar no longer cumulates them. The *Baylor Law Review* published a complete cumulation in 1966 and supplemented it six years later.[2]

The State Bar maintains a continuing legal education program which includes institutes for the practicing attorney and a series of practice books for Texas lawyers. Recent additions to the program are tape cassettes with lectures on current developments in the law. In the development stage is a computer-based legal research system similar to the one now in operation in Ohio.

Notes

1. TEX. REV. CIV. STAT. ANN. art. 320a-1 (1959).

2. 18 BAYLOR L. REV. 195-368 (1966); the remainder of the issue includes an account of judicial commentary on the canons, plus a summary of the opinions classified as to subject. Supplemented at 23 BAYLOR L. REV. 679 (1972).

Bibliography

Proceedings of the Texas Bar Association. Annual. 40 vols. 1882–1922. Imprint varies.

Supreme Court of Texas. *Rules Governing Admission to the Bar of Texas.* Austin, 1974.

Texas Bar Journal. Austin: State Bar of Texas, 1939–.

Texas Law Review. Bar Association number. Annual. Austin: Texas Law Review Inc., 1923–1938.

10. Miscellaneous Books for Texas Law Libraries

In addition to the sources discussed here, the attorney will naturally depend on such normal tools of his profession as digests, encyclopedias, law reviews, and formbooks, to say nothing of texts and treatises. The bibliography for this chapter will furnish a list of texts, but a few comments may be in order as to the standard sets needed for the everyday practice of law.

Since the *Southwestern Reporter* lacks a companion digest such as those available for nearly all other units of the National Reporter System, the *Texas Digest* is the main index to case law.[1] Its coverage includes all published cases from Texas courts and all published federal cases originating in Texas. It is similar in every respect to other Key Number digests.

Texas Jurisprudence has been superseded by *Texas Jurisprudence Second*, which began publication in 1960 and was eventually completed eight years later. In some respects the older set was preferable; it was a thorough and scholarly work, and many attorneys still keep some of the volumes on their shelves. The treatment of oil and gas law was particularly good. However, the second series added several new topics and provides some extra features, such as forms of pleading and procedural advice on such routine matters as adoption and divorce.

A newcomer in this area is *Shepard's Texas Law Locator*, which offers five volumes of a kind of condensed encyclopedia and five volumes of an index digest which covers statutes, regulations, and law review articles as well as cases.

The *Texas Annotations* published for the first series of ALI

Restatements are long since outdated and almost unusable. They have not been supplemented; as is true in all jurisdictions, *The Restatement in the Courts* is the only complete source of citations (see bibliography for Chapter 7).

The utility of nonlegal sources should not be ignored by the practitioner. The biennial *Texas Almanac* contains information on persons, places, institutions, officials, and events in the state, both current and historical. A table of district and county judges and court officials is particularly useful. Another feature is a list of names and addresses for the officers of hundreds of statewide associations, including many of interest to lawyers: certified public accountants, city attorneys, chiefs of police, legal secretaries, court reporters, and dozens of others.

Another useful reference source is the two-volume *Handbook of Texas*, published by the State Historical Society in 1952. It contains brief articles on biographical, historical, geographical, and other aspects of the state. Its account of the development of the legal system is condensed but accurate; also included are histories of important cases, information on legal education in the state, and similar material. A supplement is in preparation.

The bibliography for this chapter lists a great many books on various fields of law, written primarily for the Texas attorney. Few law offices will need all of these, but each may prove useful to some. Those listed in earlier chapters are not repeated here.

Almost all of the titles are still in print, but some no longer listed by the publishers are included where no current substitutes are available. These works, as well as those privately printed, may usually be located through a used-book dealer.[2]

Notes

1. There was at one time a *Texas and Southwestern Digest*, which first appeared in about 1923. Supplementation continued until 1959; however, since there was no cumulation, but merely a series of annual volumes, its utility was greatly limited. It ceased publication and has not been re-established.

2. The most likely dealers for Texas books are John R. Mara Law Books, 5628 Richmond Avenue, Dallas, Texas 75206, and Claitor's Book Store, Box 239, Baton Rouge, Louisiana 70821.

Bibliography

Andrus, Jack L. *Municipal Tort Liability in Texas*. Austin: Institute of Public Affairs, 1962.

Bailey, Edward Weldon. *Texas Law of Wills*. Texas Practice, vols. 9–10. Kansas City: Vernon, 1968.

Barton, Robert. *Texas Peace Officers' Manual*. Kerrville, 1973.

Bell, Charles H. *Texas Real Estate*. Rev. ed. Houston: Gulf Publishing Co., 1973.

Branch's Annotated Texas Penal Code. 2d ed. 5 vols. Rochester: Lawyers Co-op, 1956. 3d ed., 3 vols. to date, 1974–.

Davenport, Harbert, and J. T. Canales. *The Texas Law of Flowing Waters*. Brownsville, 1949.

Davis, Norris G. *The Press and the Law in Texas*. Austin: University of Texas Press, 1956.

Erisman, Fred. *Manual of Reversible Errors in Texas Criminal Cases*. 2d ed. Longview: Texas Law Book Publishers, 1974.

Flahive, Terrence, and Ron Ogden. *Texas Compensation Manual*. Austin, 1975.

Gilbert, Arch B. *Texas and Federal Estate and Tax Planning*. Atlanta: Harrison, 1974.

——. *Texas Estates Manual*. Looseleaf. Dallas: Mara, 1963.

Hamilton, Robert W. *Business Organizations*. Texas Practice, vols. 19-20. Saint Paul: West, 1973.

Handbook for Texas Law Enforcement Officers. Austin, 1972.

Hinsley, J. C. *Handbook of Texas School Law*. 4th ed. Austin: Steck-Vaughn, 1968.

Hospitalization of the Mentally Ill in Texas: A Handbook for the Attorney Ad Litem. Austin: Hogg Foundation, 1970.

How to Live and Die with Texas Probate. Rev. ed. Houston: Gulf Publishing Co., 1974.

Hutcheson, Jim. *Manual for Juvenile Court Judges*. Austin: Civil Judicial Council, 1973.

Hutchins, Wells. *Water Rights in Texas*. Austin: Board of Water Engineers, 1961.

Jentz, Gaylord. *The Texas Uniform Commercial Code*. Rev. ed. Austin: Bureau of Business Research, 1972.

Jordan, Walter E. *Modern Texas Discovery*. 2 vols. San Francisco: Bancroft-Whitney, 1974.

——. *Trial Handbook for Texas Lawyers*. San Francisco: Bancroft-Whitney, 1971.

Labor Law Manual for Texas Workers. Rev. ed. Austin: AFL-CIO, 1967.

Lange, Fred A. *Land Titles and Title Examination*. Texas Practice, vols. 3-5. Kansas City: Vernon, 1961.

Ledbetter, Jack W. *Texas Family Law*. 3d ed. Austin: Bureau of Business Research, 1970.

Lieck, Charles J. *Lieck's Legal Trial Aid*. 2d rev. ed. San Antonio: Lieck and Co., 1959.

Lowe, L. Hamilton. *Remedies: Injunctions and Other Extraordinary Proceedings*. 2d ed. Texas Practice, vols. 6-6A. Saint Paul: West, 1973.

McClung, Paul J. *Jury Charges for Texas Criminal Practice*. Rev. ed. Fort Worth, 1973.

——. *Lawyers' Handbook for Texas Criminal Practice*. Rev. ed. Fort Worth, 1973.

MacCorkle, Stuart A. *The Texas City: Its Power to Zone*. Austin: Institute of Public Affairs, 1955.

McCormick, Charles T., and Roy R. Ray. *Texas Law of Evidence*. 2d ed. Texas Practice, vols. 1-2. Kansas City: Vernon, 1956.

McLeaish, Donald C. *The Laws of the State of Texas Affecting Church Property*. Canon Law Studies, no. 405. Washington, D.C.: Catholic University of America Press, 1960.

Mahany, Maxwell M. *Texas Taxes*. Dallas: Wilkinson Printing Co., 1946.

Mitchell, Arthur, and Arch Gilbert. *Methods of Practice*. Texas Practice, vols. 11-16. Saint Paul: West, 1970-1971.

Moorhead, Dean. *Texas Wills Manual*. Looseleaf. Louisville: Blakemore and Gathright, 1960. Distributed through Texas Bankers Association members.

Moses, Ray E. *Criminal Defense Sourcebook: A Texas Lawyer's Guide*. Houston: Lakeland Press, 1974.

——. *Scientific Proof in Criminal Cases: A Texas Lawyer's Guide*. Houston: Lakeland Press, 1969.

Nunn, William H. *A Study of the Texas Homestead and Other Exemptions*. Austin: Baldwin, 1931.

Oil and Gas Law. 3 vols. Austin: Texas Law Review, 1951-1959.

Rayburn, Madison. *Texas Law of Condemnation*. Houston: Texas Law Press, 1960.

Ross, Jack. *Handbook on Parole and Executive Clemency in Texas*. Austin: Board of Pardons and Paroles, 1970.

Shepard's Texas Law Locator. 10 vols. Colorado Springs: Shepard's Citations, 1974.

Smoot, Graham. *Texas Special Issues in Personal Injury Cases*. San Francisco: Bancroft-Whitney, 1957.

Solberg, Erling D. *Legal Aspects of Farm Tenancy in Texas*. College Station: Texas A&M College System, 1950.

Speer, Ocie. *Marital Rights in Texas.* 4th (Oakes) ed. Rochester: Lawyers Co-op, 1961.

State Bar of Texas. Professional Development Program:

Appellate Procedure in Texas. 1964.

Commercial Collections Manual. 1972.

Consumer Credit Law in Texas. 1970.

Creditors Rights in Texas. 1963.

Handling a Workmen's Compensation Claim. 1968.

Legal Form Manual for Real Estate Transactions. 1973.

Personal Injury Litigation in Texas. 1961.

Texas Family Code, Forms and Practice Guide. 1973.

The Texas Lawyer: Why and How to Incorporate. 1969.

Texas Pattern Jury Charges. 2 vols. 1970.

Texas Practice Guide. 2 vols. 1971.

The Texas Probate System. 1972.

Texas Association of Legal Secretaries (TALS). *Texas Law Office Handbook.* San Francisco: Bancroft-Whitney, 1970.

Texas Bankers Association. *Lending Officer's Manual: The Uniform Commercial Code in Texas.* Rev. ed. Austin, 1967.

Texas Digest. 42 vols. in 82. Saint Paul: West, 1935–.

Texas Jurisprudence Second Edition. 73 vols. San Francisco: Bancroft-Whitney, 1959–1966.

Texas Title Insurance Manual. Austin: Steck-Vaughn, n.d.

Thrombley, Woodworth J. *Special Districts and Authorities in Texas.* Austin: Institute of Public Affairs, 1959.

Thurow, Harold F. *Real Estate Law of Texas.* 7th rev. ed. Austin: Hemphill's Book Store, 1974.

Tillman, Massie. *Tillman's Trial Guide.* Austin: Steck-Warlick, 1970.

Wall, Mary Kate. *Texas Municipal Election Law.* Denton: North Texas State University, 1971.

Walton, Ralph. *Texas Law in Layman's Language.* Houston: Gulf Publishing Co., 1970.

Weatherley, Gerald. *Texas Justice and Corporation Court Manual.* Baton Rouge: Claitor's Book Store, 1964.

Woodward, M. Kenneth, and Ernest E. Smith. *Probate and Decedents' Estates.* Texas Practice, vols. 17–18. Saint Paul: West, 1971.

Workmen's Compensation Law Manual-Texas. Austin: Steck-Vaughn, 1970.

Formbooks

Elliot, Frank, and Millard Ruud. *Uniform Commercial Code Forms.* Also known as *Vernon's Texas Code Forms Annotated.* 2 vols. Kansas City: Vernon, 1968.

Kendrick, Herbert S., and John J. Kendrick, Jr., eds. *Texas Transaction Guide Legal Forms.* 10 vols. Albany: Matthew Bender, 1972.

Moffett, Dan. *Moffett's Texas Forms.* 10th ed. Austin, 1958.

Stayton, Robert W. *Texas Forms with Practice Commentaries.* 4th ed. 11 vols. Kansas City: Vernon, 1957–1962.

Texas Forms, Legal and Business. 6 vols. San Francisco: Bancroft-Whitney, 1969–1971.

TJ Forms: Pleading and Practice. 2d ed. 13 vols. San Francisco: Bancroft-Whitney, 1972–1974.

Willson's Texas Criminal Forms. 7th ed. Texas Practice, vols. 7–8. Kansas City: Vernon, 1966. New penal code supplement, 1973.

Nonlegal Reference Works

Handbook of Governments in Texas. Looseleaf. Austin: Texas Advisory Commission on Intergovernmental Relations, 1973.

Handbook of Texas. 2 vols. Austin: State Historical Association, 1952.

Texas Almanac and State Industrial Guide. Dallas: Dallas Morning News, biennial (odd years).

Texas State Directory. Austin, biennial (odd years).

Appendix A

Articles Printed in Vernon's Texas Revised Statutes Annotated

Constitution

Volume 3 (1955). Sayles, John. *Introduction to Constitutions of Texas*. Reprinted from Sayles, *Constitutions of the State of Texas . . . Annotated*. Saint Louis: Gilbert, 1888.

Civil Statutes

Volume 2 (1953). Cox, F. Lanier. *The Securities Act*.

2A (1963). O'Quinn, Trueman. *The History, Status, and Function of Cities, Towns, and Villages*.

3 (1952). Fritz, William F. *The Texas Law of Conveyancing*.

3A (1956). State Bar Committee. *Introduction to the Business Corporation Act*. Also appearing in this volume are the proceedings of the Texas Business Corporations Act Institute held at the University of Texas School of Law in 1955, containing nearly two hundred pages of commentary and advice on the act.

8 (1951). Hodges, Gus M. *Uniform Declaratory Judgments Act*.

9 (1952). McCall, Abner. *History of Texas Election Laws*.

9A (1952). Richey, Harvey M. *History and Commentary on Title 54, Estates of Decedents*.

13 (1960). Huie, William O. *The Law of Texas Community Property.*
14 (1963). King, William J. R. *History and Development of Insurance Law in Texas.*
16 (1958). Boynton, Edward Y. *Mechanics' Liens.*
17A (1955). Moorhead, Dean. *Foreword to Probate Code.*
21 (1954). Davenport, Harbert. *Texas Law of Waters.*
22 (1956). Clark, Charles E. *The Texas Workmen's Compensation Act.*

Code of Criminal Procedure

Volume 1 (1954). Stumberg, George W. *Jurisdiction and Venue in Criminal Cases.*
1 (1966). Erisman, Fred. *Introduction to the 1965 Revision.*

Penal Code

Volume 1 (1952). Morrison, W. A., and George P. Blackburn. *The Law of Principals, Accomplices and Accessories.*
1A (1952). Ford, Bert. *The Texas Liquor Control Act.*

Appendix B

Biographical Sources

Although most attorneys rarely consider the need for biographical material, its value should not be overlooked. Reaching far beyond information on an individual, the best biographies offer a very effective method of tracing the history and development of legal institutions through the life of a key figure.

Individual biographies are too numerous to list, but many sources of biographical sketches are available, with or without historical aspects. The memorials in Bar Association and State Bar publications have been mentioned; these are adequately indexed, and need only a brief search to locate. Less well known are the memorials and tributes in the *Texas Reports* and other court proceedings. Historical sketches also occur, although less frequently.

In addition, there are several collections of biographies of important figures on the Texas legal scene. This kind of book was popular in the nineteenth century and for a few years into the present one but is rarely encountered now.

Collective Biographies

Biographical Directory of the Texas Conventions and Congresses. Huntsville, 1942. Published at the direction of the legislature.

Davenport, J. Harbert. *History of the Supreme Court of Texas, with Biographies.* Austin: Southern Law Book Publishers, 1917.

De Cordova, Jacob. *Texas: Her Resources and Her Public Men.* Waco: Texian Press, 1969. Reprint of 1858 Lippincott edition.

Foote, Henry S. *Bench and Bar of the South and Southwest.* Saint Louis: Soule, Thomas and Wentworth, 1876.

Handbook of Texas. Austin: State Historical Association, 1952.

Johnson, Francis W. *A History of Texas and Texans.* 5 vols. Chicago: American Historical Society, 1914.

Kemp, Louis W. *The Signers of the Texas Declaration of Independence.* Houston: Anson Jones Press, 1944.

Kittrell, Norman G. *Governors Who Have Been, and Other Public Men of Texas.* Houston: Dealey-Adey-Elgin Co., 1921.

Lynch, James D. *Bench and Bar of Texas.* Saint Louis: Nixon-Jones, 1885.

Speer, Ocie. *Texas Jurists 1836–1936.* N.p., 1936.

Texas Reports; Texas Criminal Reports

Although considerable material of a biographical nature was printed in the early volumes of *Texas Reports*, it is not always available for research today. Many volumes now extant are reprints in which the supplementary and prefatory notes have not been preserved; others, rebound after several pages were lost, lack the first few pages. Perseverance will usually locate a complete copy in a state or university collection.

The most common items are of course the eulogies or memorials to deceased judges of the supreme court. Sometimes a ceremony held to mark the retirement of a judge furnishes a suitable occasion for a biographical sketch. Such memorials are not limited to judges, however; a governor, a clerk of the court, or a reporter may be the recipient of the tribute.

Some of the historical sketches are extremely good sources. George Paschal in particular supplied sketches, while he was the court reporter, on the history of the court. His note in volume 29 on General Sheridan's removal of the judges, his history of the Civil War years in volume 28, and the report of his own removal as reporter, in volume 31, are eloquent, if biased, descriptions of the difficulty of those years of war and Reconstruction.

Lists of attorneys admitted to practice appear in volumes 29 and 30, and at intervals there are tables of judges in chronological order; that in volume 117 includes the volumes in which their opinions are published and the reference to any memorial or tribute. Some of these tables include lists of clerks and reporters. The final such table appeared in 1963, along with a brief historical sketch of the courts, as a separately paged supplement in *Texas Decisions*, 361–362 *Southwestern Reporter, Second Series*. It contains a list of all appellate judges of the republic and state, with the dates of their terms.

Similar tables have been published in the *Texas Criminal Reports*, and many biographical notes appear there also. Frequently portraits are included with the memorial or tribute. Many of these record only the retirement of a judge or clerk, with very little accompanying information. The *Texas Civil Appeals Reports* did not offer comparable sections.

Biographical Sketches in Texas Reports

Alexander, James P. 146:632.
Baker, James A. 90:viii.
Batts, Robert L. 126:xi.
Bell, James H. 85:xii.
Bonner, Micajah H. 60:xii; 126:ix.
Brewster, Few. 156:655.
Brown, Thomas J. 107:657.
Campbell, Thomas M. 112:xiii.

Clark, George. 111:xxiv.
Collingsworth, James. 126:xxxi; 30:ix.
Connerly, Fred. 123:v.
Critz, Richard. 158:646.
Cureton, Calvin M. 135:635.
Dabney, Samuel B. 137:649.
Denman, Leroy G. 107:657.
Devine, Thomas J. 77:v.
Fly, William S. 124:v.
Gaines, Reuben R. 107:657.
Gill, Waltus H. 116 (pages not numbered).
Gould, Robert S. 98:v.
Gray, Peter W. 40:v.
Greenwood, Thomas B. 146:623.
Gregory, Thomas W. 122:v.
Hartley, Oliver C. 21:v.
Hemphill, John. 28:ix; 59:vii.
Hickman, John E. 163:i.
Ireland, John. 89:v.
Lipscomb, Abner S. 19:iii.
McCaleb, Claude. 126:xix.
Moore, George F. 60:vii.
Peeler, Anderson. 68:v.
Phillips, Nelson. 132:637.
Pierson, William. 131:633.
Ramsey, William F. 112:v.
Roberts, Oran M. 92:v.
Robertson, Sawnie. 85:v.
Sharp, John J. 150:673; 156:671.
Short, Hugh B. 125:v.
Smedley, Graham B. 153:625.
Stayton, John W. 87:v.

Sweeton, Clyde. 126:xxiv.
Taylor, William M. 158:639.
Walker, Alexander. 90:v.
West, Charles S. 66:v.
Wheeler, Royall T. 27:v; 28:v.
Williams, Frank A. 149:659.
Willie, Asa H. 92:xiii.
Wolters, Jacob F. 126:xxxv.
Yantis, James E. 111:xxi.

Note: A memorial to Judge William R. Norvell is published in a special supplement at the front of volume 453–454 *Southwestern 2d Texas Cases*.

Biographical Sketches in Texas Court of Appeals Reports *and* Texas Criminal Reports

Beauchamp, Tom L. 156:xv.
Burts, James H. 33:vii.
Calhoun, George. 150:xxv.
Campbell, Thomas M. 94:xiii.
Christian, George E. 143:xxv.
Davidson, Lloyd W. 167:xvi.
Ector, M. D. 7:v.
Graves, Harry N. 159:xvi.
Harper, Alfred J. 104:xvii.
Hawkins, Frank Lee. 153:xiv.
Jackson, Alexander M. 28:iii.
Kleberg, Rudolph. 98:xxvii.
Krueger, C. G. 152 (pages not numbered).
Lattimore, Offa Shivers. 135:xxv.

Morrow, Wright C. 144:xxv.
Ramsey, William F. 94:v.
Roberts, Oran M. 39:v.
Simkins, Eldred James. 45:v.
Smith, Thomas. 9:v.
Walker, Alexander S. 35:v.
Wheeler, C. A. 172:vi.
White, John P. 56:v.
Williams, Lud. 109:xxi.
Willson, Sam A. 30:v.
Winkler, Clinton M. 11:xi.

Appendix C

Publications in Foreign Languages

An interesting facet of Texas legal history, although of no substantive importance, is the publication of government documents in languages other than English. Since many citizens of the new republic were of course Spanish or Mexican and all settlers were accustomed to bilingual documents, it was natural that early laws and proclamations should appear in both English and Spanish. Not so well known is the fact that for many years the government took care to see that its citizens of other nationalities should be equally well served.

With vast amounts of public land available and a widely scattered population, Texas endeavored both as republic and as state to attract immigrants from Europe. The largest groups who responded to the brochures of the Bureau of Immigration came from Germany; thus it came about that for many years successive congresses and legislatures provided for publication of the laws in English, Spanish, and German, with equal numbers of copies in each language. In the decade just before the Civil War this practice was extended to publications of nearly all branches of the government, including annual reports. One edition of the Constitution of 1876 was printed in Czech, as were some immigration brochures; but, so far as is known at present, there were no Czech editions of laws. After the Civil War there was little interest in continuing the translations, and there are no existing documents in any foreign language other than Czech, German, and Spanish.

Complete references to the foreign-language documents will be found in two standard sources: Thomas Winthrop Streeter, *Bibliography of Texas*, 5 vols. (Cambridge: Harvard University Press, 1955-1960); and Ernest William Winkler, *Checklist of Texas Imprints, 1846-1860*, 2 vols. (Austin: Texas State Historical Association 1949-1963).

Appendix D

Citation Forms

Citation form is arbitrary at best, and no one rule or set of rules can be proclaimed the best in all circumstances. However, it is important to be consistent in the form used, and with that purpose in view many courts and attorneys general have issued their own guides for citations in briefs and opinions.[1] Law review editors prefer to follow the rigid and frequently confusing rules of the "Harvard Bluebook,"[2] but many attorneys shun its complexities. The editors of the *Texas Law Review* have compiled a supplement to the "Bluebook" for use with Texas materials, called *Texas Rules of Form*, which has become an influence toward standardization of citations by Texas courts and attorneys. The 1974 edition is reproduced here by permission of Texas Law Review Publications, Inc., successor in interest to the Texas Law Review Corporation, holder of the original copyright.

Texas Rules of Form

I. Texas Cases

1. SUPREME COURT

1:1. Current. The discontinuance of the official Texas Reports in 1963 necessitated a modification of the citation form for cases decided by the Texas Supreme Court. All cases decided since the discontinuance of the official reports are to be cited: Utica v. Bennett, 492 S.W. 2d 659 (Tex. 1973).

1:2. Texas Reports. Cases decided prior to 1963 are included in the official Texas Reports (first published in 1846), and the citation to these cases should contain a parallel citation to that source: McWilliams v. Muse, 157 Tex. 109, 300 S.W.2d 643 (1957). Since the Southwestern Reporter was not published until 1886, citations to cases before that date will contain only the Texas Reports citation: Peters v. Phillips, 19 Tex. 70 (1857). Care should be exercised in citing cases between 1861 and 1874, as cases decided during that period are generally not considered to be as authoritative as those previously and subsequently decided.

1:3. Supreme Court Journal. Opinions of the Texas Supreme Court are not published in the Southwestern Reporter until that court overrules the motion (or motions) for rehearing. If a case has not yet appeared in the Southwestern Reporter advance sheet, the proper citation is to the Texas Supreme Court Journal (published weekly): Jennings v. Spahn, 17 Tex. Sup. Ct. J. 63 (Nov. 10, 1973). Until September 1957 the Texas Supreme Court Journal was called the Texas Supreme Court Reporter and was cited Tex. Sup. Ct. Rptr.

1:4. Republic of Texas. The cases decided by the Supreme Court of the Republic of Texas (1840–1844) are recorded in Dallam's Digest (one volume) and are to be cited: Hunter v. Oelrich, Dallam 357 (Tex. 1840).

1:5. Disposition by U.S. Supreme Court. Any disposition by the United States Supreme Court of a case decided by a Texas court is to be indicated: Roedenbeck Farms v. Broussard, 133 Tex. 126, 127 S.W.2d 168, *appeal dismissed*, 308 U.S. 514 (1939). Caveat: While certiorari disposition is to be shown, it should be remembered that denial of certiorari ("*cert. denied*" notation) in a case does not indicate Supreme Court approval of the decision.

2. COURT OF CRIMINAL APPEALS

2:1. Current. The official Texas Criminal Reports were discontinued in 1963 with the Texas Reports, and all criminal appeals cases decided after this date are to be cited: Guzman v. State, 508 S.W.2d 375 (Tex. Crim. App. 1974).

2:2. Texas Criminal Reports. The citation of cases decided prior to 1963 is to include a parallel citation to the official Texas Criminal Reports (first published in 1876): Goliath v. State, 172 Tex. Crim. 100, 354 S.W.2d 160 (1962).

3. COMMISSION OF APPEALS

In citing cases decided by the old commission of appeals of the supreme court (1920–1945), one must necessarily ascertain whether the entire opinion of the commission was adopted or whether only the judgment was adopted or the holding approved. This information appears immediately following the report of the particular case in the Southwestern Reporter.

3:1. Opinion Adopted. When the entire opinion of the commission was adopted, the case will be found in the official Texas Reports and should be cited in exactly the same manner as though it were a decision of the supreme court. Such a case has the full authority of a supreme court decision. Every case decided by the commission after 1934 is to be cited in this fashion, since all commission opinions after this date were adopted by the supreme court until the commission was absorbed in 1945: McCrory v. Smeltzer, 132 Tex. 383, 124 S.W.2d 336 (1939). In rare instances "opinion adopted" cases are not reported in the Texas Reports: Alex v. Webb, 40 S.W.2d 72 (Tex. Comm'n App. 1936, opinion adopted).

3:2. Holding Approved. Approval by the supreme court of the

holding of a commission decision signifies that the supreme court approved the judgment and adopted each specific holding of the commission, but did not necessarily approve its reasoning. These cases do not appear in the official reports, but only in the Southwestern Reporter, and are to be cited: Texas Power & Light Co. v. Culwell, 34 S.W.2d 820 (Tex. Comm'n App. 1931, holding approved).

3:3. Judgment Adopted. When the supreme court adopted the judgment of a commission decision it approved neither the specific holdings nor the reasoning. The Texas Supreme Court currently, however, treats the holding-approved and judgment-adopted cases as having the same authority for all practical purposes. These decisions are to be cited: Savage v. Rhea, 33 S.W.2d 429 (Tex. Comm'n App. 1930, jdgmt adopted).

4. COURTS OF CIVIL APPEALS

4:1. Complete Citation. All cases decided by the courts of civil appeals should be cited only to the Southwestern Reporter (disregard the old Texas Civil Appeals Reports published from 1892 to 1911). A complete civil appeals citation must contain the reporter citation, the court of decision, the city in which the court is located, the date, and either the writ-of-error history or the subsequent history: Welsh v. Wood, 482 S.W.2d 193 (Tex. Civ. App.—Corpus Christi 1973, writ ref'd n.r.e.); Walton v. Collins, 499 S.W.2d 193 (Tex. Civ. App.—Amarillo), *aff'd on other grounds*, 500 S.W.2d 87 (Tex. 1974). Court of civil appeals opinions not appearing in reporters are cited: Phillips v. Campbell, Docket No. 51-341 (Tex. Civ. App.—El Paso, March 9, 1973) (unreported). There is a question concerning the precedential value of these unreported opinions . . . If the opinion has not yet been, but will be, reported, the preceding citation form is to be used with the substitution of the parenthetical "not yet reported."

4:2. Cities. A complete civil appeals citation should include a reference to the city in which the particular court sits since, in some areas of the law, one civil appeals court may follow a rule of law different from that followed by another. Those cities in which courts of civil appeals are located are (in order of district):

Houston (1st Dist.) (formerly Galveston)	Dallas	Waco
	Texarkana	Eastland
Fort Worth (never abbreviated)	Amarillo	Tyler
	El Paso	Corpus Christi
Austin	Beaumont	Houston (14th Dist.)
San Antonio		

The Houston courts should now be cited as: Orange v. White, 477 S.W.2d 232 (Tex. Civ. App.–Houston [1st Dist.] 1973, no writ), and Long v. Horn, 466 S.W.2d 382 (Tex. Civ. App.–Houston [14th Dist.] 1972, writ dism'd). When Texas cases are cited in out-of-state publications, reference to the city in which the court is located may be omitted, but in no case should a writ notation (4:3 *infra*) be omitted.

Prior to 1912 the courts of civil appeals were designated by districts instead of cities. It is not necessary to show the district in which the court was located during this period.

4:3. Writs. Unless the rule of subsequent history (4:5 *infra*) applies, a complete civil appeals citation *must* include the writ-of-error history to determine how the Texas Supreme Court has disposed of the particular case. Therefore, it is imperative that the Texas Writ of Error Table be examined in connection with every civil appeals case cited. To ascertain the disposition of civil appeals cases decided since the latest edition of the Writ of Error Table, one should consult the pink tables in the most recent Southwestern Reporter advance sheet. If the disposition does not yet appear in the pink tables, the first page of the most recent Texas Supreme Court Journals should be consulted to ascertain whether application for a writ has been made and whether there has been any recent disposition of it by the supreme court.

The following forms are to be used in citing the filing, absence, or disposition of an application for writ of error:

1. writ granted	5. writ dism'd jdgmt cor.	8. writ dism'd by agr.
2. writ ref'd	6. writ ref'd n.r.e.	9. no writ
3. writ dism'd	7. writ ref'd w.o.m.	10. writ filed
4. writ dism'd w.o.j.		

The table [in Chapter 7] should help explain the meanings of some of the above citation forms.

It should be noted that the currently used "writ dism'd" notation does not inform the reader whether the dismissal was by agreement of the parties or by direction of the court. This information can be indicated parenthetically (*see* Whitebook § 27:1–3).

The Texas Supreme Court has recently begun to include explanations, per curiam, why some applications for writ of error were refused by the court. Such a decision should be cited according to the rules for subsequent history (4:5 *infra*).

4:4. No Writ History. A case having no writ history should be cited: Coates v. De Garcia, 456 S.W.2d 291 (Tex. Civ. App.—San Antonio 1970, no writ). If the civil appeals decision is very recent and an application for writ of error has been filed, but not yet acted upon, or filed and the writ granted, but has not been disposed of by the supreme court, notation to that effect is to be made: Unthank v. Rippstein, 380 S.W.2d 155 (Tex. Civ. App.—Amarillo 1964, writ filed).

4:5. Subsequent History. The subsequent history of a civil appeals case is given for any disposition by the Texas Supreme Court after granting a writ or by the U.S. Supreme Court; the history on remand and any denial of rehearing are omitted unless relevant to the point for which the case is cited. The complete citation should appear: Regan v. Cordelia, 445 S.W.2d 906 (Tex. Civ. App.—San Antonio), *rev'd on other grounds*, 453 S.W.2d 342 (Tex. 1973). Note that the year of the lower court's decision need not be given if identical to the year of the supreme court's decision.

When the Texas Supreme Court has written, per curiam, an explanation why it has refused an application for writ of error, the decision should be cited: Conner v. Witschey, 505 S.W.2d 324 (Tex. Civ. App.—Fort Worth), *writ ref'd n.r.e. per curiam*, 506 S.W.2d 44 (Tex. 1974).

When the Texas Supreme Court reverses a civil appeals court decision without hearing oral argument, pursuant to TEX. R. CIV. P. 483, the court will issue a per curiam opinion that can be cited in a subsequent history as follows: Hardhat v. Ajax Constr. Co., 497 S.W.2d 967 (Tex. Civ. App.—Dallas 1972), *rev'd per curiam*, 499 S.W.2d 232 (Tex. 1973).

See Whitebook § 1:5:1 for other abbreviations that can be used in subsequent histories.

5. DISTRICT COURTS (UNREPORTED CASES)

The citation form for Texas district court cases (none of which are reported) is as follows: State v. Topless Club, Crim. No. 75227, Dist. Ct. of Travis County, 126th Judicial Dist. of Texas, May 7, 1974; Renfro v. Weeks, Civ. No. 83621, Dist. Ct. of Rusk County, 4th Judicial Dist. of Texas, Nov. 9, 1972.

6. MISCELLANEOUS

6:1. White and Willson. The old Texas Court of Appeals (1876-1891) decided a limited number of civil cases which were privately edited by White and Willson. These cases will be found in the four volumes of Texas Court of Appeals, Civil Cases, and are to be cited: Gibbons v. Braden, 1 White & W. 128 (Tex. Ct. App. 1883).

6:2. Texas Criminal Reports. Decisions of the old Texas Court of Appeals, which comprise the first twenty-nine volumes of the criminal reports, are to be cited: Martin v. State, 21 Tex. Ct. App. 1 (1886).

6:3. Texas Reports. Cases referred to the old commission of appeals (1876–1891) by the supreme court and the court of appeals are included in the official Texas Reports and are to be cited: Taylor v. Huck & Co., 65 Tex. 238 (1885). All of these opinions were adopted by the supreme court.

6:4. Posey. The cases that attorneys agreed should be referred to the commission of appeals, as distinguished from those referred by the supreme court and the court of appeals (*see* 6:3 *supra*), are reported in the two volumes of Posey's Unreported Cases (1879–1884) and are to be cited: McCarthy v. Martin, 1 Posey 143 (Tex. Comm'n App. 1880).

II. Texas Constitutions

7. CURRENT CONSTITUTION

In a citation of the present constitution, adopted in 1876, the date is not included: TEX. CONST. art. II, § 2.

8. PRIOR CONSTITUTIONS

The date is always included when a constitution other than the one in force is cited: TEX. CONST. art. III, § 3 (1869).

III. Texas Statutes

9. CURRENT STATUTES

All current statutes should be cited to *Texas Revised Civil Statutes Annotated* (the Black Statutes) and the annual pocket parts that supplement the bound volumes.The legislature is continuing to revise and codify Texas statutes; to date five of an eventual twenty-eight codes have been reformulated. These five new codes (Business and Commerce Code, Water Code, Education Code, Family Code, and Penal Code) employ a decimal section system, and all references to articles have been eliminated. The date following each citation is the year in which the volume was published, which varies with each code or compilation.

9:1. Vernon's. Citations to the bound volumes of the statutes described above are to be in the following form:

TEX. REV. CIV. STAT. ANN. art. 4619, § 3 (1960).
TEX. BUS. & COMM. CODE ANN. § 16.14(a) (1) (A) (i) (1968).
TEX. BUS. CORP. ACT. ANN. art. 206A (2) (1956).
TEX. CODE CRIM. PROC. ANN. art. 36.07 (1965).
TEX. EDUC. CODE ANN. § 33.09 (1972).
TEX. ELECTION CODE ANN. art. 3.55 (1962).
TEX. FAMILY CODE ANN. § 22.42 (1974).
TEX. INS. CODE ANN. art. 3.55 (1963).
*TEX. PENAL CODE ANN. § 2.18 (1974).
**TEX. PENAL CODE AUX. LAWS art. 11, § 3 (1973).
TEX. PROB. CODE ANN. § 27 (1956).
TEX. TAX.-GEN. ANN. art. 3.01 (1960).
TEX. WATER CODE ANN. § 17.52 (1972).

*Some portions of the old Penal Code that were neither incorporated into the new Penal Code nor repealed were transferred to *Texas Revised Civil Statutes Annotated*. For a table showing the disposition of those sections, see Tex. Laws 1973, ch. 399, at A-197.

**Chapters 11 and 18 of the old Penal Code are undergoing recodification as a separate Texas Alcoholic Beverage Code and a Texas Parks and Wildlife Code. In the interim, they will be found in a temporary publication, *Texas Penal Code Auxiliary Laws*, which retains the same article and section numbers as the old Penal Code. This temporary publication will be updated annually until the recodifications appear.

Statutes appearing in the pocket parts of the bound volumes are to be cited in the same manner as above, but the word "Supp." and the year appearing on the title page of the supplement are to be substituted for the date of the compilation: TEX. REV. CIV. STAT. ANN. art. 489d, § 6 (Supp. 1966).

Many minor codifications are located in and cited as articles of *Texas Revised Civil Statutes Annotated.* The Texas Mental Health Code is an example; it begins at article 5547 and is cited: TEX. REV. CIV. STAT. ANN. arts. 5547-36 (1958).

The Texas Uniform Commercial Code has been incorporated into the Texas Business and Commerce Code. For clarity and easy cross reference, the Texas UCC should be noted parenthetically: TEX. BUS. & COMM. CODE ANN. § 2.403 (Tex. UCC 1968). Note that sections of the Texas Uniform Commercial Code do not always correspond to sections of the Uniform Commercial Code.

Citation problems arise when two or more articles are to be cited. The following forms are suggested:

a. When two or more articles are cited, but no sections are involved: TEX. REV. CIV. STAT. ANN. arts. 456, 476, 486 (1959).

b. When two different articles are to be cited, each with section number: TEX. REV. CIV. STAT. ANN. art. 34, § 1, and art. 35, § 44 (1959).

c. When more than two articles, each with section number: TEX. REV. CIV. STAT. ANN. art. 235, § 14, art. 241, § 20, and art. 245, § 1 (1959).

d. When two or more articles are to be cited, some with a section number and some without: TEX. REV. CIV. STAT. ANN. arts. 45, 47, art. 123, § 1, and art. 135, § 3 (1959).

e. When more than two articles, each with section number and one or more appearing in the Supplement: TEX. REV. CIV. STAT. ANN. art. 235, § 14 (1959), art. 241, § 20 (1959). and art. 245, § 1 (Supp. 1965).

Note that order is determined by article number rather than by the date of the volume in which the article appears.

9:2. Texas Session Laws. If a statute is currently in effect, but has not yet appeared in a pocket supplement of the Black Statutes, the proper citation is to the session law, which can be found in Vernon's Texas Session Law Service: Tex. Laws 1965, ch. 679, § 7, at 1563. The page number should always be included.

9:3. Future Codifications. The Texas Legislative Council is currently working on formal codification of the Texas statutes. When and if approved by the legislature, these codifications are to be cited by abbreviated code name, section number, and date. For example: TEX. AGRIC. CODE § 28.32 (19xx).

10. STATUTES NO LONGER IN EFFECT

If a statutory provision referred to is no longer in effect (because of repeal, substitution, amendment, etc.), only the official session law is to be cited, even if the law appears in the current annotated codification: for general laws, cite Tex. Laws 1929, ch. 234, § 6, at 494; for other laws, cite by name—*e.g.*, Tex. Laws, Local & Spec. 1929, ch. 173, § 8, at 28. If the provision was promulgated at a specially called or extra session, the citation is to include such information: Tex. Laws, 1st Spec. Sess. 1957, ch. 34, § 1, at 99.

11. STATUTES IN EARLIER REVISIONS AND CODIFICATIONS

If it becomes necessary to cite a statute appearing in one of the three earlier official revisions, the following forms are to be used:

a. Tex. Civ. Stat. art. 221 (1879).

b. Tex. Rev. Civ. Stat. art. 1039 (1895).

c. Tex. Rev. Civ. Stat. art. 4362 (1911).

d. Tex. Code Crim. P. art. 120 (1879).

12. STATUTES PRIOR TO 1898

When it becomes necessary to cite a session law promulgated prior to 1898, a parallel citation to H. Gammel, Laws of Texas 1822–1897 is to be included: Tex. Laws 1885, ch. 43, § 17, at 120, 9 H. GAMMEL, LAWS OF TEXAS 662 (1898).

Laws passed by the first legislature (1846) do not have chapter numbers. They must be cited by title and page number: Tex. Laws 1846, An Act To Define the Boundaries of Montgomery County § 2, at 222, 2 H. GAMMEL, LAWS OF TEXAS 396 (1898).

13. COMMENTS AND COMMENTARIES ON STATUTES; LEGISLATIVE RECORDS

Appearing intermittently in the *Texas Revised Civil Statutes Annotated* are short comments by the bar and commentaries by legal scholars on specific statutes. Commentaries that include the name of the author are to be cited: Huie, *Commentary on the Community Property Laws of Texas*, 13 TEX. REV. CIV. STAT. ANN. 44 (1960). Short comments by the bar, with no designated author, are to be cited: TEX. REV. CIV. STAT. ANN. art. 5547-36, comment (1958).

Legislative records are to be cited as follows: Greetings to President Wilson, TEX. H.R.J. 609 (1919); Message from Governor Sayers, TEX. S.J. 12 (1901).

IV. Quasi-Statutory Material

14. RULES

14:1. Current Rules. The Texas Rules of Civil Procedure are procedural rules promulgated by the Texas Supreme Court. If currently in force, they are to be cited as codifications: TEX. R. CIV. P. 97(d).

14:2. Rules No Longer in Force. Rules no longer in force are to be cited to the latest official source in which they appear: TEX. R. CIV. P. 195 (1941).

14:3. Commentaries on Rules. Commentaries on the rules are to be cited as follows: Calvert, *The Application for Writ of Error*, TEX. R. CIV. P. ANN. 469.

15. ORDERS, REGULATIONS, AND RULINGS

15:1. Attorney General Opinions. Beginning in 1939 (Gerald C. Mann, Attorney General) a consecutive numbering system was adopted for all opinions. From 1939 to 1947 each opinion number was prefaced by the letter "O" (not to be confused with the number "zero"). Since 1952 (after the term of Attorney General Price Daniel, who employed the letter "V" for "Victory") the opinion numbers have been prefaced by the initials of the attorney general rendering the opinion.

Citations to these opinions are to include the opinion number and the year in which the opinion was issued: TEX. ATT'Y GEN. OP. NO. H-311 (1974). String citations should be arranged with the most recent opinion first, as follows: TEX. ATT'Y GEN. OP. NOS. M-15 (1969), WW-135 (1957), S-07 (1953).

Prior to 1939 there existed no standardized numbering system to identify the opinions of the attorney general. Citations to these opinions are to include the name of the official to whom the opinion is directed and the *exact* date of the opinion. A parallel citation to the Biennial Report of the Attorney General of the State of Texas is to be included: TEX. ATT'Y GEN. OP. (To Honorable Tom Finty, Jr., Jan. 28, 1927), 1926–1928 Tex. Att'y Gen. Bien. Rep. 262.

15:2. City Attorney Opinions. City legal departments are often called upon to write opinions on legal matters concerning, for example, application of local ordinances and legal consequences of action by other branches of the city government. Although different cities use different filing and classification systems, citations to these opinions should include the city and state, subject matter of the opinion, exact date, the official to whom the opinion is directed, and the legal department file number, if any: Houston, Tex., Legal Dep't Opinion, City Enforcement of Private Deed Restrictions (To Mayor Louis Cutrer, June 18, 1963) (L.D. File No. 1864).

15:3. Agency Material. Although it would be impossible to standardize all of the material published by different state commissions and agencies, the goals of conciseness and clarity must be considered when devising citation forms to apply to individual pamphlets, memoranda, leaflets, etc. The following are intended as examples only, and are by no means exhaustive.

15:3:1. Texas Railroad Commission. The railroad commission is divided into four divisions, each with different citation forms for its orders and rules. The division will be obvious from the subject matter and need not be identified unless an order from the transportation division is referred to in a proceeding dealing with oil and gas. The following examples are proper citations for the Oil and Gas Division. This general form will be followed in other divisions, but any peculiarities should be handled according to that division's citation forms.

a. Orders are cited: Docket No. 5-6050, Requiring George T. Williams to Properly Plug the Garth (01566) Lease Corsicana Shallow Field, Navarro County, Texas, May 19, 1974.

b. Rule 37 cases are cited: Case No. 36,440, Joe R. Doe's Application to Drill his No. 3 Windham, May 31, 1974.

c. Rules are cited: Rule 44, Statewide Rules, Tex. R.R. Comm'n, Oil & Gas Div.

15:3:2. Other Rulings and Regulations. A citation example for rulings and regulations promulgated by state regulatory agencies is as follows: Tex. Water Comm'n, Rules, Regulations, and Modes of Procedure 2 (1964 rev.).

16. TEXAS CODE OF PROFESSIONAL RESPONSIBILITY

16:1. Current State Bar Code. The following citation forms should be used when citing rules or code provisions for the State Bar of Texas (located immediately following TEX. REV. CIV. STAT. ANN. art. 320a-1 [1973]) or when citing opinions by the State Bar's Committee on Interpretation: (1) State Bar of Texas, Comm. on Interpretation of the Code of Professional Responsibility, opinion 73 (1973) [hereinafter cited as State Bar of Texas Opinions]; (2) State Bar of Texas, Rules and Code of Professional Responsibility, DR 5-105(C), EC 5-17 (1971) [hereinafter cited as State Bar of Texas Code] ; (3) State Bar of Texas, Rules and Code of Professional Responsibility, art. XII, § 34(c)(3) (1970).

16:2. Former Canons of Ethics. When citing to the old rules, canons, or opinions, use the following cite forms: (1) State Bar of Texas, Comm. on Interpretation of the Canons of Ethics, opinion 1 (1946); (2) State Bar of Texas, Rules and Canons of Ethics, canon 10 (1957); (3) State Bar of Texas, Rules and Canons of Ethics, art. XII, § 34 (1957).

V. Secondary Material

17. BOOKS

17:1. Commonly Cited Books. Citations to books should include author, title, date of publication, editor (if any), and edition (if any other than first edition). For complete rules of citation see Whitebook § 9. Some commonly cited books by Texas authors are: 1 R. HAMILTON, TEXAS BUSINESS ORGANIZATIONS § 23 (1973); G. HODGES, SPECIAL ISSUE SUBMISSION IN TEXAS 124 (1959); 1 C. MCCORMICK & R. RAY, TEXAS EVIDENCE § 41 (2d ed. 1956); O. SPEER, MARITAL RIGHTS IN TEXAS § 302 (4th ed. 1961); 3 H. WILLIAMS & C. MEYERS, OIL AND GAS LAW § 631 (1965); C. WRIGHT, FEDERAL COURTS § 26, at 75 (1963).

17:2. Encyclopedias. The only encyclopedia of Texas law is *Texas Jurisprudence*, which is to be cited: 59 TEX. JUR. 2d *Venue* § 10 (1964); 59 TEX. JUR. 2d *Venue* § 10 (Supp. 1974).

17:3. Essays and Theses. Essays compiled in book form should be cited to the compilation and its date, as well as to the author and title of the essay: Johnson, *Discovery Procedures on Behalf of the Plaintiff*, in STATE BAR OF TEXAS, PERSONAL INJURY LITIGATION IN TEXAS § 4.1, at 161 (1961); King, *Appeals to the County Court*, in STATE BAR OF TEXAS, APPELLATE PROCEDURE IN TEXAS § 3.1 (1964). If an essay or thesis is not published, it should be cited with reference to where it can be found: Ray, Constitutional Limitations on Local and Special Laws in Texas 18 (unpublished thesis in The University of Texas School of Law Library).

17:4. Form Books. The following are standardized citation forms for commonly used Texas form books: 2 STATE BAR OF TEXAS, TEXAS PATTERN JURY CHARGES (1970); R. STAYTON, TEXAS FORMS § 4054 (1960); 4 TEX. JUR. FORMS 47, *Depositions* § 4:35 (1954); S. WILLSON, TEXAS CRIMINAL FORMS § 2372 (W. Morrison & T. Blackburn eds. 1956).

18. PERIODICALS

18:1. Law Reviews. Abbreviations of law reviews published in Texas are as follows:

a. American Journal of Criminal Law: AM. J. CRIM. L.
b. Baylor Law Review: BAYLOR L. REV.
c. Houston Law Review: HOUS. L. REV.
d. Journal of Air Law and Commerce: J. AIR L. & COMM.
e. St. Mary's Law Journal: ST. MARY'S L.J.
f. South Texas Law Journal: S. TEX. L.J.
g. Southwestern Law Journal: SW. L.J.
h. Texas International Law Journal: TEX. INT'L L.J.
i. Texas Law Review: TEXAS L. REV.
j. Texas Southern University Law Review: TEX. SO. U.L. REV.
k. Texas Tech Law Review: TEX. TECH L. REV.
l. Urban Law Review: URBAN L. REV.

Cite, *e.g.*, Pillai, *Consumer Protection in Aviation Rate Regulation*, 38 J. AIR L. & COMM. 215 (1972); Yudof, *The Property Tax in Texas Under State and Federal Law*, 51 TEXAS L. REV. 885 (1973).

18:2. Other Periodicals. For complete information on periodical citations see Whitebook § 11. Other citation examples of Texas periodicals are: Calvert, *Constitutional Revision*, 36 TEX. B.J. 1126 (1973); Hodges, *Recent Cases on Contribution and Indemnity*, 13 DALLAS BAR SPEAKS 44 (1950); Ryan, *Texas Energy Industries, 1972*, TEX. BUS. REV., June, 1972, at 120; Tex. Water Report, June 10, 1965, at 4.

19. CONFERENCE AND INSTITUTE PROCEEDINGS

Conference and institute proceedings that are bound as such are to be cited with the name of the sponsor of the institute first, followed by the number of proceedings, if any, and the type or title of institute; finally, the date (in parentheses) is to follow the page designation of the reference: SW. LEGAL FOUNDATION 9TH INST. ON OIL & GAS LAW & TAX. 35 (1958). A specific essay or paper by an identified author is to be cited as an essay (*see* 17:3 *supra*): Huie, *Some Recent Developments on the Law of Oil & Gas*, in ABA PROCEEDINGS—MINERAL & NATURAL

RESOURCES 148 (1960); McCall, *Inter-Basin Transfers of Water*, in UNIV. OF TEXAS PROCEEDINGS ON WATER LAW 125 (1959); Sealy, *The Effect of Conservation Laws and Practices Upon the Express Provisions of Oil and Gas Leases*, in ROCKY MT. 7TH ANN. MINERAL-LAW INST. 1 (1962).

If the paper or essay appears in a special series of bound proceedings, the citation to the volume should correspond to the volume's title: McKay & Woodward, *Corporate Buy and Sell Agreement Forms*, in 4 TEXAS INSTITUTES 7TH ANN. TAX. CONF. 177 (1959); Walker, *The Problems of the Small Tract Under Spacing Regulations*, in 57 TEX. BAR ASS'N PROCEEDINGS 157 (Texas L. Rev. 1938).

When a record of the proceedings appears in a statutory compilation, a parallel citation should be included to this effect: Trotti, *Should an Existing Corporation Adopt the Act?*, in TEXAS BUSINESS CORPORATION ACT PROCEEDINGS 15 (1953), 3A TEX. REV. CIV. STAT. ANN. 455-56 (1956).

If a paper or address delivered at a proceeding has not been published in any form, it is to be cited as follows: Address by Walter Koch, Mineral Law Section Meeting, Texas State Bar Convention, July 2, 1965.

In citations to institute proceedings or conferences, the following abbreviations (other than those sanctioned by the Whitebook § 1:1:2) may be used: Conf. (Conference); Univ. (University); Inst. (Institute); Ann. (Annual); Tax. (Taxation).

20. REPORTS, STUDIES, AND BULLETINS

Reports, studies, and bulletins published in pamphlet form should be cited in the same form as that used for books (*see* 17:1 *supra*), except that pamphlets of extremely limited circulation are to be cited with the exact date. *See generally* Whitebook § 9:1.

Examples of citations to numbered series of bulletins or reports are: Keith, Methods of Constitutional Revision 3, 1949

(Bureau of Municipal Research Information Bull. No. 3); Tex. Water Comm'n Circular No. 62-06, Oct. 1962; Tex. Water Comm'n, Development of Ground Water in the El Paso District, 1962 (Bull. No. 6204).

Governmental agencies and institutional authors should be cited in the same manner as any other author: HOUSE GENERAL INVESTIGATING COMM., 58TH LEGISLATURE OF TEXAS, REPORT ON SLANT-HOLE INVESTIGATIONS 83 (1963); TEX. COMM'N ON HIGHER EDUCATION, REPORT TO THE GOVERNOR AND THE LEGISLATURE (1962); TEX. RESEARCH LEAGUE, SCHOOL DISTRICT STRUCTURE IN TEXAS 28 (1955). *See* Whitebook § 9:1:1 for special rules for abbreviation of institutional authors.

Annual and other regular reports are cited in abbreviated form. Always name the agency first, and do not separate the agency from the title by a comma. The number of the report is given as if it were a volume number. *See generally* Whitebook § 9:6. An example citation of an annual report is as follows: 36 TEX. CIV. JUD. COUNCIL ANN. REP. 107 (1964).

VI. Order of Citation

For order of signals and order of citations within a signal see Whitebook § § 28–29. Citations of cases decided by the same court should be arranged in reverse chronological order; for this purpose the fourteen courts of civil appeals are treated as one court. The following order is to be observed in citations containing decisions of more than one Texas court:

a. Texas Supreme Court
b. Texas Court of Criminal Appeals
c. Texas Commission of Appeals
d. Texas Courts of Civil Appeals
e. Texas District Courts

Notes

1. *See, for example*, UNIFORM CITATIONS FOR OPINIONS, BRIEFS AND CORRESPONDENCE (Austin: Attorney General of Texas, 1967), usually reissued under the name of each attorney general when he takes office; J. Greenhill, *Uniform Citations for Briefs*, 27 TEX. B. J. 323 (1964).

2. A UNIFORM SYSTEM OF CITATION. 11th ed. Cambridge: Harvard Law Review, 1967.

Index